The Happy
VOLUNTEER

Enriching Your Life
through Volunteering

A Guide to
Personal Fulfillment

DONALD RUHL

Library of Congress Cataloging-in-Publication Data

Ruhl, Donald L.

The Happy Volunteer

Enriching Your Life Through Volunteering

A Guide to Personal Fulfillment

ISBN: 978-0-692-03106-3

Library of Congress Control Number: 2015911862

First published in 2015

Turnstone Press, LLC

Rye NH

Graphic design by Raleigh Design

Editor: Sarah Raleigh

Printed in the United States of America

Dedication

This book is dedicated to my wife, Ellen Ruhl,
and to our daughters, Beth and Heather.

About the Author

Dr. Donald Ruhl is an organizational consultant specializing in not-for-profit organizations. He is Dean Emeritus of the College at Northern Essex Community College (Mass.) and the former President of Garrett Community College in Maryland. Dr. Ruhl served for fifteen years as the Executive Director and then President of the Greater Haverhill Chamber of Commerce in Massachusetts. Dr. Ruhl has had extensive experience both as a volunteer and in working with other volunteers in a broad range of not-for-profit organizations. This book is the result of those experiences.

Dr. Ruhl is the co-author of the pioneering book, *Breakthrough Management for Not-For-Profit Organizations: Beyond Survival in the 21st Century* (Brown and Ruhl-Praeger-2003). Dr. Arthur Levine, former President of Teachers College, Columbia University, said of the book, "Brown and Ruhl have managed to produce an extraordinary volume that could become a new standard text both for individuals considering the not-for-profit field and those who are already professionals in the field."

Dr. Ruhl's most recent book, *Survival Fundraising for Small Not-for-Profits*, was published by Turnstone Press, LLC.

Dr. Ruhl and his wife, Ellen, reside in New Hampshire and Florida.

Acknowledgements

This book is dedicated to my wife, Ellen Ruhl, and to my daughters Beth and Heather. My wife's continuing support and encouragement were critical to the successful completion of this book.

The ideas presented and discussed in books are frequently the result of experiences which have taken place over an extended period of time. Mentors are of great importance in the continuing development and refinement of these ideas.

The author has been extremely fortunate to have had an outstanding group of mentors during his career. This group includes: Jack Armstrong, Ken Benne, Harold Bentley, Joseph Bevilacqua, Paul Bevilacqua, Charles Billups, William Cavallaro, John Dimitry, Eugene DuBois, Ferd Ensinger, Joseph Giampa, Malcolm Knowles, Arthur Levine, Stuart Marshall, Barry Oshry, Gene Phillips, Robert Ramsey, John Ravekes, Lowell Trowbridge, Ed Veasey, and Robert Webber.

Special thanks go to Sarah Raleigh of Raleigh Design for her ideas and creativity in bringing clarity and interest to the layout of this book. Her contributions have added greatly to the readability and impact of the book. Sarah has also been involved in the overall publication process of the book. The support of her husband, John Raleigh, in this publishing effort is also greatly appreciated.

Deborah Downes of ColorPage, a division of Tri-State Associated Services, Inc., has done an excellent job of guiding this book through the printing and production process. Her commitment to bringing this project to a successful completion is very much appreciated.

Table of Contents

Introduction

Who Should Read this Book?

You should read the book if:

- You want to experience more personal satisfaction, joy and meaning in your life.
- You want to discover and do work that you feel passionately about.
- You have thought about being a volunteer but for one reason or another haven't become involved.
- You are currently a volunteer who wants to get more out of the volunteer experience.
- You are attempting to discover your authentic self.
- You are trying to clarify your goals in life.
- You are at a stage in life where you are looking for relevant, productive, worthwhile learning experiences.
- You are interested in advancing your career through relevant new learning experiences.
- You are interested in changing your career.
- You are interested in gaining significant leadership experience with minimum risk.
- You are involved in recruiting volunteers.
- You work with volunteers.
- You lead or manage an organization in the not-for-profit, for-profit, or public sector.
- You are a counselor or practitioner in the human development profession.

Background and Reasons for Writing this Book

The author strongly believes that the process of volunteering provides a great way for each of us to enrich our lives. Being a volunteer has the potential to do the following things for you:

- Increase your zest for and enjoyment in life.
- Enhance your sense of worth and self-esteem.
- Help you to better understand yourself and find your passions.
- Increase your creativity.
- Grow and develop your spiritual self.
- Increase your emotional and social intelligence.
- Learn about different cultures and how to effectively relate to them.
- Make available a wide range of learning opportunities.
- Develop new skills and competencies.
- Make new friends and develop new contacts.
- Make a difference in a cause that is important to you.

Being a volunteer can open up a truly amazing world of opportunities for you. The purpose of this book is to make it easy for you to learn about and take advantage of these opportunities. The volunteer experience offers you possibilities for enriching your life that most people never dream about.

Most of the books written about the volunteer experience talk about how to recruit, manage, and lead volunteers. This book speaks directly about the tremendous benefits received by the volunteer in the process of volunteering.

The major focus of the book is on volunteering in not-for-profit organizations, including religious institutions. Many people do volunteer work in the public and for-profit sectors as well, and the discussions in this book are also relevant to these organizations.

Nearly 25 percent of all jobs in the United States are currently in the not-for-profit sector. The fact that these organizations are amazingly diverse in nature provides an unusually rich environment for volunteer experiences. Not-for-profit organizations are found in many different fields of human activity. Among these are: the arts, athletics and recreation, business, education, the environment, health, the political arena, religion and the spiritual life, and social service endeavors.

The broad range of fields of interest of not-for-profit organizations and the availability of mentors in these fields greatly enhances the personal enrichment process in the volunteer experience. Added to this is the fact that not-for-profit organizations are private organizations governed by boards comprised of volunteers who serve as role models for volunteer enrichment and contribution.

The commonality of purpose that ties together all not-for-profit organizations is that they are involved in improving some aspect of the human condition. Many of these organizations are involved in improving the human condition at the most basic and fundamental level, which further enhances the potential and importance of the volunteer learning experience. Not-for-profit organizations are indeed the land of opportunity for personal enrichment, fulfillmcnt, and contribution for volunteers.

One of the great things about the process of volunteering is the fact that people of all ages can get a tremendous amount of value from the experience.

This book discusses age-specific benefits in some detail. People volunteer for many different reasons and these reasons frequently change with age. It is the author's hope that this book will serve to encourage people of all ages to become volunteers, thereby greatly enriching their lives while helping others.

Each of us has different needs at different times in our lives and the volunteer experience provides a wonderful way, because of the broad range of options, to help us meet these needs. Experiencing the satisfaction, personal fulfillment, and fun of volunteering creates an excitement and energy that you can build upon as you try new things and experience new opportunities in different stages of your life.

A major emphasis of this book is placed on the way in which the volunteer views the volunteer experience. A volunteer is urged to view herself or himself as a full-fledged member of the staff who is doing important work and to be pro-active in pursuing the volunteer experience. Part of the tremendous personal satisfaction one receives as a volunteer comes from knowing that the work being accomplished is of critical importance to the organization and in many cases essential to its very survival.

The author of this book believes that a volunteer should make every effort to look at and learn from as many aspects of the work environment as possible. Special emphasis should be given to learning about those things in the organization that are especially relevant to the goals and objectives of the volunteer. An example of this would be serving on a volunteer board of directors in order to learn about how the various parts of the organization work together to accomplish its mission. This is but one example of the special benefits that can be available to those who participate as volunteers.

It is important to note that the special status of volunteers in an organization can result in opportunities that might not normally be available to employees in paid positions. This book includes a discussion of these advantages and how to benefit from them. A list of some of these advantages appears below:

Some Advantages a Volunteer May Have Over a Paid Employee

- An increased number of available work experiences.
- An opportunity to work in a greater number of functional areas.
- A greater opportunity to structure the work environment.
- The chance to observe the overall organization in a policy-making role through service on a board of directors.
- The availability of a greater number of mentors.
- Being perceived as a helper rather than a competitor.
- The respect received from others because of the dedication and commitment demonstrated by working without financial compensation.
- The desire on the part of people to meet and talk to volunteers; to discover what motivates them.
- An increased opportunity to get honest feedback concerning one's performance.

In order to maximize these advantages in the learning process, a volunteer needs to be pro-active in working to create appropriate experiences with his or her learning goals clearly in mind. Being as clear as possible about your learning goals in the volunteer experience is of the utmost importance. Remember to keep in mind the old adage that you won't be able to get someplace if you don't know where you want to go. One of the purposes of this book is to help you determine as clearly as possible what you hope to personally get out of the volunteer experience as you participate in the process of serving others. The fact that you are serving others enhances the value you receive with regard to your own learning and personal fulfillment. One of the great things about being a volunteer is that it is a win-win situation for the volunteer and for those being served. The volunteer is a winner and the recipients of the services are winners.

This book focuses on the many benefits received by the volunteer in terms of personal self-fulfillment, career development, and the realization of life-time goals. Utilizing one's creativity, understanding the importance and significance of the cultures of which each person is a part, and forming a set of values are emphasized as important aspects of the volunteer learning experience. It is important to remember that the volunteer learning experience includes the overall relationship between the volunteer and the environment with which he or she is interacting.

The bottom line of this book is to point out the tremendous benefits of being a volunteer and to urge you, the reader, to enrich your life by actually becoming a volunteer. Not only will you truly become "The Happy Volunteer," but you will also encourage others to become "Happy Volunteers" thereby advancing and expanding the great American volunteer tradition.

Organization of the Book

The book is divided into five chapters:

- Chapter 1: Experiencing the Many Personal Benefits of Volunteering
- Chapter 2: Realizing the Maximum Benefit from Your Volunteer Experiences
- Chapter 3: Using Volunteer Experiences to Advance Your Career
- Chapter 4: Achieving Life Goals through Volunteering
- Chapter 5: Finding the Right Volunteer Opportunities in the Right Organizations

Each chapter begins with an introductory section that helps to provide a framework and point of reference for the information provided in that chapter. The chapters are divided into subsections each of which deals with important ideas for making your volunteer experiences more rewarding for you. At the conclusion of each chapter is a section entitled, "Being a Happy Volunteer — Questions to ask yourself after reading this chapter." This section is designed to help you implement the ideas that are presented in the chapter in your experiences as a volunteer. Each chapter also contains several pages which are titled, "Wisdom from the Happy Volunteer." These pages highlight some of the most important ideas for making your experiences as a volunteer as personally enriching and rewarding as possible.

It is the hope of the author that the reader will find the information in each chapter to be interesting, informative, and useful. The success of each chapter depends upon the manner in which you, the reader, take action as a result of reading it. The continuing purpose of this book is to get you to take action, to experience the wonderful things that can happen to you to enrich your life as a result of being a volunteer. The author wants this to be a book that will be of great personal benefit to you.

Suggestions for Reading the Book

Each chapter should help you to experience more fun and meaning in your life by showing you how to become part of the great American volunteer tradition. Each chapter provides useful and helpful information about the tremendous personal benefits that you can receive as you pursue the many opportunities available to you as a volunteer.

As you read each chapter ask yourself:

- What are the most important things in this chapter that will help me meet my learning and self-enrichment goals as I help to improve the lives of others?

- How can I use this chapter to better understand, sharpen, and focus my personal enrichment goals?

- Who can I discuss this chapter with, who could best help me to think about and implement the most important and relevant ideas in this chapter as they pertain to my goals for the volunteer experience?

- What kind of specific organizational experiences would provide me with the best opportunities to implement the ideas contained in this chapter?

- What mentor or mentors would be most helpful in making the ideas in this chapter come alive?

- What specific action steps can I take utilizing my ideas about the information in this chapter to achieve my personal enrichment goals in the volunteer process?

It is the author's hope that as you read this book each chapter will increase your motivation to become a volunteer. The desired end result is that you will actually do it; that you will participate in the volunteer experience.

As you read each chapter, imagine yourself personally experiencing the benefits discussed in that chapter as you help to improve some aspect of the human condition. Create a picture in your mind of the specific contributions that you could make as a volunteer in a setting that is of interest to you, in a cause that excites and motivates you. The author deeply appreciates your reading this book. What is of the essence, however, is that your reading of the book results in your taking action to experience the many benefits of being a volunteer.

And Finally...

The author believes that the characteristics in a volunteer that will provide the greatest joy, fulfillment, and personal growth for the volunteer and the greatest benefit for those being served are:

- A strong sense of personal self-worth.
- A belief that one is capable of making a difference for the better.
- A strong desire to continue to learn.
- A belief in human potential; one's own and that of others.
- Behavior that is pro-active rather than re-active; taking the initiative to make things happen.
- An openness to new experiences.
- A mind-set that is optimistic rather than pessimistic.

Wisdom from the
HAPPY VOLUNTEER

"Being a volunteer can open
up an amazing world
of opportunities for you."

"Volunteer work may be
the most important work
that you do in your lifetime."

- The ability to recognize excellent performance, study it, and learn from it.

- The ability to understand the culture of the organization in which one is working; the way of life of its people.

- The ability to keep personal growth objectives clearly and continuously in mind.

Each of us possesses some of these characteristics and we can use them to experience the fun, joy, meaning, personal growth, and fulfillment that comes from our participation as volunteers as we work to improve the world in which we live.

The author wishes you the very best as you embark on the incredibly rewarding adventure of the volunteer experience.

Chapter 1 —
Experiencing the Many Personal
Benefits of Volunteering

Before You Get Started

- Approach your volunteer experiences fully realizing that through them you can experience real happiness, joy, and personal fulfillment.

- Be fully aware of the fact that the work you are doing is important; you are part of a world-wide community of volunteers working to make the world a better place in which to live.

- Determine as clearly as possible, in as much detail as possible, what your goals and objectives are for your volunteer experiences. Keep these goals and objectives continuously in mind.

- Be aware of the fact that there are many opportunities to be a volunteer in a broad range of fields of interest.

- Be pro-active in pursuing your volunteer experiences; take the initiative to make your volunteer experiences incredibly satisfying, worthwhile, and life-changing.

- Fully understand and utilize your unique role as a volunteer to make your volunteer experiences as worthwhile and personally rewarding as possible.

- Observe and learn from as many aspects of the organization as possible that relate to your goals and objectives.

- Realize that volunteer experiences can be of great value at different stages in your life in meeting your changing needs for personal growth, fulfillment, and happiness.

Overcoming the Barriers to Volunteering

Despite the fact that there are so many wonderful life-changing benefits to being a volunteer, there continues to be a large number of people who are missing out on these benefits. If you are one of these people, the author urges you to think about what is keeping you from experiencing the rich rewards of being a volunteer.

A number of perceived barriers to volunteering are identified below. When these barriers to volunteering are carefully examined, it is obvious that some of them have absolutely no basis in fact and that others can be easily overcome with a minimal effort and a little planning. Almost all of these barriers to volunteering are based on inadequate or incorrect information that results in faulty pre-judgments and stereotyped thinking. Some of this stereotyped thinking about volunteering is reinforced by values existing in our contemporary society.

Some Perceptual Barriers to Being a Volunteer

A belief that:
- Successful people don't volunteer.
- Volunteer work is comprised of menial, mindless, boring tasks.
- It isn't important because you are not being paid monetarily to do it.
- There isn't time to do it.
- Volunteering is only for "do-gooders."

- Volunteers get no respect; their efforts won't be recognized.
- Volunteers have no specific responsibilities.
- It is unimportant because we don't have to do it.

Let's consider each of these personal barriers to volunteering and see if they make sense when we look closely at them.

Successful people don't volunteer

Think about the people you know who are actively engaged in volunteer activities. Are these individuals successful in their paid positions? Are they respected in their work lives and in the communities in which they live? If they are currently enrolled in high school, college, or other educational institutions, are they successful students? There is an old saying that 20% of the people do 80% of the work. Are the volunteers you know in the 20% group? Successful people tend to be open to new experiences, to be curious, to be creative and innovative, and to want to make things happen. An analysis of social service organizations such as the Rotary Club, Kiwanis, Exchange Club, Soroptimists, etc., demonstrates clearly that successful individuals with these characteristics do a great deal of volunteer work. Service organizations are dramatic examples of successful people who are volunteers in action.

Volunteering involves doing menial, mindless, boring tasks

The truth of the matter is that volunteering can involve some of the most important work you will ever do in your life. This is the case because volunteering in not-for-profit organizations involves work whose product is improving

Wisdom from the
HAPPY VOLUNTEER

"When you volunteer, view yourself as a full-fledged member of the staff who is doing important work."

"Being pro-active is essential to your success as a volunteer."

the human condition. The product is the creation of human happiness, self-fulfillment, and contribution. The benefits to the volunteer are tremendous because of the great variety of volunteer opportunities which are available that provide the most significant kinds of experiences for personal enrichment and growth at different life stages when they are needed the most. Volunteers of different ages have different needs and the range of choices for volunteer work fits beautifully into what is most needed at a particular point in time. It is of critical importance that the volunteer take the initiative in seeing to it that the volunteer work being done is important and that it is directly related to his or her learning and enrichment goals. Volunteers are in demand and have many choices concerning where they will volunteer. Menial, mindless, boring work should be the last thing that they should be doing.

It isn't important because you are not being paid monetarily to do it

One of the greatest rewards in volunteering is to be able to help advance causes that are of personal importance to you, that you couldn't contribute significantly to on your own. Volunteering to join with others in a cooperative effort to improve the human condition in an area that is important and personally rewarding to you allows you to greatly increase your chances of achieving your personal goals for that area of human endeavor.

This volunteer involvement for which you are not being paid monetarily may be more personally satisfying, enriching, and important to you than work for which you are being paid. It may also be the case that working for this particular cause is not a realistic possibility for you in a paid position.

A great advantage of volunteer positions in relation to paid positions is the opportunity to participate in experiences that are personally rewarding to you that wouldn't be available if you were being paid to do them.

There isn't enough time to do it

High performers are individuals who learn to spend their time doing things that make a significant difference for the better. They effectively manage their time and spend it doing things that are important. Learning to make decisions about what is important in life and what is not important can be greatly facilitated by volunteering in not for-profit organizations.

The process of working with people who are frequently dealing with issues of personal survival, with basic and fundamental issues of living one's life, helps to provide the volunteer with a conceptual framework that is extremely useful in weighing basic time management issues. Successful time management involves choices about how one will spend one's time. Learning to use one's time in productive ways is especially enriching and rewarding. For most individuals, the problem is not not enough time, but rather the effective utilization of time.

Some of the best prospects for volunteer participation and involvement are individuals who believe they don't have enough time to do it. This is because involvement as a volunteer has the possibility of providing them with the joy of learning how to spend their time on things of the first importance. Showing individuals who think they don't have enough time to volunteer that through volunteering they will learn how to have more time to do the things that are most important to them is an exciting challenge for the people who lead and manage not-for-profit organizations.

Volunteering in not-for-profit organizations is fertile ground for developing personal strategies for effective time management.

Volunteering is only for "do-gooders"

This is not true. Volunteering is for people who are interested in self-improvement, self-enrichment; in experiencing more meaning, happiness, joy, and self-fulfillment in their lives. It is for people of all ages. Volunteering is for individuals who are interested in realizing their potential. It is for people who want to advance their careers and achieve life-time goals. The fact that volunteers are frequently involved with helping people serves to enhance and enrich the variety of reasons for which they volunteer.

Volunteers get no respect — their efforts won't be recognized

The reality is that volunteers are usually highly respected for their commitment to a cause that is important to them. They serve as a model of dedication and commitment by contributing time, effort, and energy to help an organization carry out its mission without receiving financial compensation. Many not-for-profit organizations would be unable to survive without the continuing involvement of volunteers. These organizations recognize the importance of volunteer contributions in a variety of ways. They realize that recognition is an especially important motivator for volunteers since they are not receiving financial compensation for their services.

Volunteers have no specific responsibilities

Volunteers do have specific responsibilities. It is important that these responsibilities be defined as clearly as possible before a volunteer begins his or her involvement with an organization. It is highly desirable that these responsibilities be spelled out in a written agreement in order to be certain that all the parties involved have agreed upon expectations. This agreement should include such items as the number of hours to be worked, the locations where the work can be performed, the opportunities for new assignments, opportunities for performance feedback, the availability of mentors, and the manner in which the volunteer experience will be supervised. Volunteers should be treated in this agreement as full-fledged members of the staff.

It is unimportant because we don't have to do it

One of the great things about doing volunteer work is that we are able to make choices concerning what we want to do and where we want to do it. The volunteer doesn't have to volunteer but chooses to become involved. This freedom of choice provides the volunteer with a special opportunity to do things that make a significant difference for the volunteer and for others. Many volunteers discover that the work they choose to do turns out to be as important as any work they have ever done. It is a fact that one's greatest achievements frequently occur as a result of doing things that are not required of us.

Rather than being a barrier to volunteering, the fact that you don't have to do it should serve as a powerful motivator to become involved. This is because there is the potential to do something really important that is personally very satisfying and rewarding. Volunteering provides the individual with the freedom to explore and experience a wide range of growth producing opportunities while also being of service to others.

Having examined some of the common barriers that keep people from experiencing the life changing benefits of volunteering, let's look now at the many personal benefits of being a volunteer. The title of this book, *The Happy Volunteer — Enriching Your Life Through Volunteering: A Guide to Personal Fulfillment*, speaks directly to the tremendous opportunities for personal growth and fulfillment that are possible through the process of volunteering.

Volunteering is a win-win process. The volunteer is a winner and the individuals being served are winners. What a wonderful thing it is to experience the many benefits of being a volunteer as you work to improve some aspect of the human condition. The focus of this book is volunteering in not-for-profit organizations. All of these organizations are in the human improvement business. Volunteering in public and private sector organizations can, of course, also be highly rewarding to the volunteer and to the organization in which the volunteer is contributing his or her services.

This chapter focuses on the personal enrichment benefits of volunteering. These benefits can provide the foundation for increased happiness, joy, personal fulfillment, and a greater sense of personal meaning and empowerment. These personal enrichment benefits are:

- Enhanced Self-Esteem
- Finding Your Passions
- Strength of Character
- Greater Creativity
- Understanding of Diverse Cultures
- A Broader Perspective
- Increased Concern for the Human Condition

Wisdom from the
HAPPY VOLUNTEER

"The volunteer experience includes
the overall relationship between the
volunteer and the environment in which
the volunteering takes place."

"Learning about the culture and
sub-cultures of the organization
in which you are volunteering is one
of the most fascinating aspects
of the volunteer experience."

Chapter 2 will discuss the action steps that you, as a volunteer, can take to realize the maximum benefit from your volunteer experiences. In Chapter 3 we will deal with the career benefits of being a volunteer and in Chapter 4, the life goal benefits of volunteering will be discussed. Chapter 5 will discuss the process for finding the right volunteer opportunities in the right organizations.

The Personal Enrichment Benefits of Volunteering

Enhanced Self-Esteem

Volunteering in not-for-profit organizations is a great way to increase one's sense of self-confidence and self-worth. Nathaniel Brandon identifies these two attributes as the key components of self-esteem in his book, *The Six Pillars of Self-Esteem*. Having the sense that you have the personal resources to deal with life's challenges and that you are a person of worth is important in experiencing personal fulfillment and happiness. In turn, high self-esteem is essential to building satisfying and productive relationships with other people. In order to respect and value other people you must first respect and value yourself. It is highly unlikely that a person who perceives himself or herself as having little value will perceive other people as having value.

The mission of the not-for-profit organization is improving some aspect of the human condition. An important part of this mission is the building of self-esteem in its clients since self-esteem serves as the foundation for the self-improvement of these clients. The not-for-profit organization is in the self-esteem building business. Being involved in some aspect of this process is a good way to build one's own self-esteem. The process of building self-esteem is reciprocal in nature. There is a win-win relationship as the people involved in the self-esteem building process relate to and support each other.

Finding Your Passion

A piece of advice that one frequently hears is to pursue those things in your life that you feel passionately about. The idea is that if you do this you will be successful. The problem for many people is discovering their passion. It seems that there are lots of people who don't appear to be passionate about anything. Volunteering in not-for-profit organizations is a great way to discover those things that you feel passionately about in your life. It is a great way to find out what is of the first importance to you. The volunteer experience provides you with the opportunity to try out a number of things of potential interest and to observe, first hand, the outcomes that are achieved. If this isn't possible you may want to consider finding another place to volunteer.

The volunteer experience should enable you to observe people dealing with a range of basic issues of human survival, growth, and opportunity. This process is important in helping you to discover more about yourself and about the things you feel passionately about. Having a passionate commitment enables you to do your best and to move ahead in the process of realizing your potential. Passionate commitment inspires others and provides you with a tremendous amount of satisfaction and joy.

One of the important aspects of feeling passionately about some undertaking is that it provides the motivation to continue your efforts in difficult times and to work hard to bring these undertakings to completion. Many people have excellent ideas, but far fewer people successfully implement their ideas. Feeling passionately about a cause or project that is especially important to you and having the staying power to successfully bring it to completion is an incredibly satisfying experience. Passionate commitment is an important part of an individual's ability to realize his or her potential and to achieve career and life goals.

Strength of Character

Wisdom, originality, honesty, trustworthiness, fairness, loyalty, and compassion are examples of important virtues that constitute our character. Volunteering in not-for-profit organizations allows one to observe the building of character as people deal with some of the most basic issues of living. This is frequently an environment where a single volunteer can make a great deal of difference in the lives of people. Relating to people who are dealing with fundamental survival issues is character building for the volunteer who is involved in the process. The non-threatening status of the volunteer often facilitates an openness of interaction that is character building for all of the parties who are involved. A sense of community is established with trust as its centerpiece.

The success of volunteers in an organization depends to a large extent on perceptions of their actual performance and trustworthiness. Does the volunteer do what is promised? Can the volunteer be depended upon? The volunteer's authority comes not from a specific job slot on the organization chart but rather from other's perceptions of his or her abilities and strength of character as observed through actual performance. This reliance on self rather than upon the authority that comes from one's position on the organization chart builds character in the volunteer. Acting in a

Wisdom from the
HAPPY VOLUNTEER

"Volunteering can help you develop
character traits that will enable you to
live your life with greater understanding,
confidence, courage, and joy."

"Reliance on self rather than upon
the authority that comes from
one's position on the organization chart
builds character in the volunteer."

trustworthy manner is at the heart of giving the volunteer involved a sense of integrity and value as a human being.

Greater Creativity

In the volunteer process, the volunteer does not usually appear on the organization chart. The volunteer therefore has to be creative in reaching agreement concerning his specific job responsibilities and in gaining credibility through the utilization of his personal strengths and his actions to successfully implement these responsibilities. He or she has to depend to a considerable extent on his or her own ingenuity to get the job done. Opportunities to develop and use creativity are further enhanced by the fact that many different functions in not-for-profit organizations are frequently performed by volunteers, thereby making available a range of possibilities with which one can become involved. An additional factor encouraging a volunteer's creative development is the reality that many not-for-profit organizations have fewer resources with which to get the job done. This makes the creative use of these resources essential.

The creative possibilities available to a volunteer in an organization that respects and understands the value of the contributions of volunteers lay the groundwork for experiences that are exciting, stimulating, and personally fulfilling.

There can be great joy in developing and exercising one's creativity. It is a heady experience to deal with a variety of challenges in new and different ways, to consider things from different perspectives, and to develop alternate solutions. Most of us have a reservoir of creative capacity that can be utilized for the benefit of ourselves and others. Steps in developing, using, and maximizing your creative potential in the volunteer experience will be discussed in greater depth in the next chapter of this book.

Understanding of Diverse Cultures

One of the most powerful concepts to understand when interacting with other people is the powerful influence that the cultures and sub-cultures in which these people live have upon their behavior. Clyde Kluckhohn, the Harvard anthropologist, in his book, *Mirror for Man*, defines culture as "the way of life of a people." When we talk about culture, we are talking about a shared set of values, beliefs, norms, and assumptions. Many of these do not appear in writing and are passed on from generation to generation. This makes them even more powerful. The behavior of individuals is sometimes difficult to understand without a working knowledge of the cultural context within which it takes place. Learning to appreciate the distinctiveness and richness of different cultures is one of the great pleasures in living one's life. It is also a necessity if one is to function effectively in an increasingly global society.

Not-for-profit organizations are generally rich in cultural diversity. Many newcomers to the United States, as well as other countries, are clients of not-for-profit organizations. This is especially true immediately following their arrival to their new place of residence. Not-for-profit organizations assist many individuals in the process of adjusting to life in a new culture. The process of people from one culture inculcating the values, beliefs, norms, and assumptions of a new culture provides a rich environment for the study of culture for a volunteer. The fact that many of the people involved are dealing with basic societal issues further increases the learning experiences of the volunteer. If you are interested in learning more about the nature and power of culture, then volunteering in a not-for-profit organization would seem to be a good place to begin this process.

A Broader Perspective

The clients of not-for-profit organizations are involved in dealing with a wide range of issues which vary greatly in importance. Volunteers in these organizations have the opportunity to view both the larger more important issues, and the smaller less important issues with which these clients are dealing. Volunteers have the opportunity to see the big picture and the interconnected parts of which it is composed, within the context of the organization's mission or purpose. Volunteering on a board of trustees can be especially useful in this regard.

The ability to understand which issues and decisions are of the first importance and which are of lesser importance is, of course, a critically important life skill. One of the great joys in living is to be able to view one's actions within a broader context that makes sense and provides it with meaning. The volunteer experience can be a wonderful way to help develop the competencies required to view both the whole and its parts.

In this process it is important that the volunteer view the volunteer experience within the context of the overall organization including both its internal and external environments. Just as we as individuals interact with the environment in which we live, so do organizations interact with the external environments in which they operate. The volunteer experience of viewing both the internal and external environments of the organization enables the volunteer to develop a broader and more comprehensive framework for thought and action.

Concern for the Human Condition

The common thread running throughout all not-for-profit organizations is the concern for improving some aspect of the human condition. Volunteers play a critically important part in many of these efforts. They find themselves directly involved with strategies and actions designed to ameliorate or solve challenging personal and societal problems. These experiences serve to increase the awareness and sensitivity of the volunteer to the extent and range of the societal improvement issues that require attention. Many volunteers develop a sense of identification with, and compassion for, the individuals with whom they work who are attempting to improve the quality of their lives. In addition, many volunteers begin to realize that their efforts are part of a worldwide effort to improve the global society.

In order to facilitate this feeling of a "community of volunteers," it is important that various forms of interaction take place between volunteers in a range of not-for-profit organizations. This feeling of working with other volunteers to achieve outstanding results in moving the society ahead provides the volunteer with a feeling of pride and accomplishment which results in a sense of meaning and personal worth.

It is a heady experience to see individuals you are working with grow and develop before your eyes. Volunteers are motivated by psychological and social factors, not through financial compensation. Having the opportunity to be involved in helping individuals, groups, organizations, and the society at large move ahead and resolve their problems is one of the major benefits in being a volunteer in a not-for-profit organization.

Being a Happy Volunteer

Questions to ask yourself after reading this chapter:

What are the most important ideas in this chapter that will help me meet my learning and self-enrichment goals as a volunteer?

What individual or individuals would be best able to help me implement these ideas?

What kinds of specific organizational experiences would provide me with the best opportunities to implement what I have learned in this chapter?

What action steps can I take to achieve my goals using the information presented in this chapter?

Chapter 2 —
Realizing the Maximum Benefit from Your Volunteer Experiences

In Chapter 1 we discussed the general enrichment benefits that are available to a volunteer in the volunteer experience. The general enrichment benefits which were identified were: enhanced self-esteem, finding your passion, strength of character, greater creativity, understanding diverse cultures, a broader perspective, and increased concern for the human condition. In Chapter 3 we will deal with the career benefits of being a volunteer, and in Chapter 4 the life goal benefits of volunteering will be discussed. Chapter 5 will discuss the process for finding the right volunteer opportunities in the right organization.

In this chapter we will focus our attention on the action steps that you, as a volunteer, can take to realize the maximum benefit from your volunteer experiences. These action steps are:

- Have clear goals and mutually agreed upon expectations.
- Be pro-active.
- Build upon your special status as a volunteer.
- Choose great mentors.
- Exhibit trustworthy behavior.
- Utilize your creative potential
- Learn from the overall organization.

Wisdom from the
HAPPY VOLUNTEER

"Put more meaning and fun in your life! Be part of the great American volunteer tradition and have a terrific time helping yourself and others!"

"Volunteering is for people who are interested in experiencing more meaning, happiness, joy, and self-fulfillment in their lives."

- Participate in a variety of experiences.
- Interact with and learn from the organization's clients.
- Learn about community dynamics and community building.

Action Steps to Realizing the Maximum Benefit from Your Volunteer Experiences

Taking these action steps will not only increase your sense of personal well-being and your commitment to the work you are doing as a volunteer, but will also result in an increased contribution on your part to the clients of the organization who are being served. The increased satisfaction you receive as a volunteer will be reflected in the results you achieve. Your joy in helping others to succeed will open up continuing opportunities for you to enrich your own life. Volunteering increasingly becomes a win-win relationship. As you grow as a person through your volunteer experiences, you are able to contribute more to the people you serve. In addition, your experiences as a volunteer will help to provide you with the self-esteem and personal competencies which will be of great value to you in achieving your career and life goals.

Have Clear Goals and Mutually Agreed Upon Expectations

Having clear goals is essential if you are to realize the maximum benefit from the volunteer experience. It is important that your goals be kept in mind as various volunteer experiences develop. New goals may emerge and old goals become less important. Both short and long-term goals should be kept in mind.

It may be useful for you to develop a personal goals assessment inventory prior to becoming involved as a volunteer, and to review this inventory from time-to-time as the volunteer experience progresses. Following is an example of such an inventory. It can be easily modified to meet your unique needs.

Your Personal Goals Assessment Inventory

At the present time I am interested in being a volunteer for the following reasons:

- ❏ Meet interesting people
- ❏ Learn specific skills
- ❏ Meet new friends
- ❏ Be part of a group
- ❏ Try new things
- ❏ Participate in new job experiences
- ❏ Develop new ideas
- ❏ Develop new frames of reference
- ❏ Find more intellectual stimulation
- ❏ Pursue a special interest
- ❏ Deepen and broaden my education
- ❏ Become a more active person
- ❏ Give back to society
- ❏ Make a difference for the better
- ❏ Develop more compassion for others
- ❏ Support a specific organization
- ❏ Support a specific person
- ❏ Continue a family tradition
- ❏ Get involved in the community
- ❏ Advance my career
- ❏ Learn to identify common interests
- ❏ Become a better negotiator

- ❏ Learn to build win-win relationships
- ❏ Make business contacts
- ❏ Improve my communication skills
- ❏ Improve my logical reasoning ability
- ❏ Learn to take calculated risks
- ❏ Become a better problem solver
- ❏ Identify and build on personal strengths
- ❏ Increase my sense of self-esteem
- ❏ Develop my interpersonal competencies
- ❏ Enhance my artistic ability
- ❏ Learn more about myself
- ❏ Learn how to influence other people's behavior
- ❏ Meet people with other points of view
- ❏ Learn a specific recreational skill
- ❏ Learn about a different culture
- ❏ Have more fun in life
- ❏ Develop my sense of humor
- ❏ Become more adventuresome
- ❏ Increase and use my creativity
- ❏ Contribute to religious institutions
- ❏ Develop a broader perspective
- ❏ Advance causes I couldn't advance on my own
- ❏ Overcome specific fears
- ❏ Get out of a rut
- ❏ Learn how to be a change agent
- ❏ Learn a new language
- ❏ Earn college credit
- ❏ Receive recognition for my achievements
- ❏ Be of service to people
- ❏ Strengthen my religious faith
- ❏ Contribute to a specific cause

In addition to a volunteer having clear goals for the volunteer experience, it is important that there be mutually agreed upon expectations on the part of the volunteer and the individuals with whom he or she will be working. This will go a long way in helping both the volunteer and the organization to experience a win-win relationship. Using a written volunteer-organization agreement can be extremely helpful in clarifying mutually agreed upon expectations. This written agreement can be revised as the volunteer experience progresses, and modified as the individuals involved feel is appropriate.

The volunteer-organization agreement might include items such as the following: the length of the agreement, the process for selecting assignments, locations where the work can be performed, flexibility in hours, the kind of work to be performed, opportunities for increased responsibilities, the availability of mentors, forms of recognition, professional development opportunities, opportunities for feedback concerning the volunteer's performance, and opportunities to provide input to the organization.

The initial agreement between you, as a volunteer, and the organization, is of great importance in providing the framework that allows you to experience the maximum benefit from the volunteer experience. Clarity of mutual expectations is most important. Openness and honesty are important. Continuing discussion and feedback are essential. You need to be pro-active in this relationship as well as a self-directed learner.

Be Pro-Active

After you have established specific goals concerning what you want to contribute to and get out of the volunteer experience, it is essential that you be pro-active in pursuing these goals. It is up to you to maximize the wonderful opportunities available to you as a volunteer. You need to take charge of this process. Don't sit around and wait for things to happen. Take the initiative to make them happen. Following are a number of suggestions for being effectively pro-active in maximizing the specific benefits you are seeking from your experiences as a volunteer.

- Establish a productive relationship with at least one mentor who can serve as a continuing resource for you.

- Insist on volunteer opportunities that include important work.

- Work out a clear agreement about what you expect and what is expected of you in the volunteer experience.

- Observe excellent performance, study it, and learn from it.

- Seek out people who possess special competencies that are of interest to you, get to know them, and learn from them.

- Experiment with new and different ways of doing things.

- Try to figure out what are the underlying values of the organization in which you are volunteering.

- Create a list of the most important things you learn each week as a volunteer that relate to your goals.

- Request new assignments in order to secure new goal-related experiences.

- Observe the factors in the organization that turn people on and the factors that turn people off.

- Build win-win relationships with members of the paid staff.

- Get to know clients of the organization.

- Observe the interaction that takes place between the organization and its clients.

- Learn as much as you can about the overall organization and its mission.

- Look for projects that you can be involved with from beginning to end.

- Know when to move on.

Building Upon Your Special Status as a Volunteer

Being a volunteer has a number of advantages as opposed to being a paid employee in an organization. It is important that you build upon these advantages if you want to get the most out of your experiences as a volunteer.

These advantages center around the fact that people in the organization will tend to be interested in why you are volunteering and what you hope to accomplish in the process. They will want to know more about you and will probably feel at ease in communicating with you since you will most likely not be seen as someone who is competing with them for a better job or other form of advancement. People like to talk about themselves and the work they do if they can do so in a relationship of mutual trust. Volunteers, because of their non-threatening status, provide the opportunity for them to talk about themselves and their life in the organization in an open and confidential manner. This provides a wonderful opportunity for a volunteer to learn about various aspects of an organization and what makes it tick. It also provides a great opportunity to learn about the cultural dynamics of the organization such as its formal and informal structure, its leadership and decision-making processes, and its motivational dynamics.

In order to capitalize on the available feedback from the paid staff as well as clients and suppliers of the organization, a volunteer has to be clear about what he or she is interested in getting out of the volunteer experience. The goals have to be clear and sharply defined and the questions that are asked have to be designed to secure the desired information.

A major advantage of being a volunteer, as opposed to being a paid employee, is that one frequently has access to people in the organization who would not be available in the same manner if one were in a formal paid position.

Top level managers are often interested in talking to volunteers because they represent an outside perspective, provide a non-threatening sounding board, and are contributing their time, effort, and energy without receiving financial compensation.

Individuals who possess specialized skills and competencies in the organization are also often interested in talking to volunteers who are interested in gaining information about their specific areas of expertise. These individuals often serve as excellent mentors for volunteers. Again, the volunteer provides a sounding board for the specialist to talk about what he or she is doing to an interested and motivated listener.

Another advantage that a volunteer frequently has in an organization is the opportunity to become involved with a project that he or she can participate in from beginning

Wisdom from the
HAPPY VOLUNTEER

"Volunteering helps you to tap into your inner resources in order to achieve goals that are important to you."

"Volunteering can be of great assistance in helping you to identify, build on, refine, and utilize your personal strengths."

to end. This is important because the volunteer has the opportunity to view the process in its entirety. Many people begin projects but fail to help to bring them to completion. Being able to do so is a great experience for the volunteer and becomes an important part of the value of the volunteer experience when it is assessed by other people on the resumé of the volunteer.

Choose Great Mentors

When we talk about choosing great mentors we are referring to identifying and building productive relationships with individuals who can help us achieve our personal enrichment and learning goals in the volunteer experience. These individuals may be located inside or outside of the organization in which you are volunteering. These relationships may be of a relatively short duration or in some cases may continue for an extended period of time. The impact of the mentoring process may be highly specific in nature or may be broad-based in nature. Some of our mentors may have a major influence on our lives while others may have a helpful but much less important impact upon us. In some cases these mentors will serve as role models to help us achieve our learning and self-enrichment goals as we work as volunteers.

Following are some characteristics that you may want to look for as you seek mentors who will help you to maximize your learning and self-enrichment goals in the volunteer process. Working with these mentors should also help you to contribute in more important ways to the clients you are serving as a volunteer. As you examine the characteristics identified below, think about the ones that you consider to be most important in mentors that you would like to work with in your volunteer experiences.

Characteristics of a Good Mentor

Personal Qualities

Someone who:

- Cares about you.
- You trust.
- You respect professionally.
- You have a good feeling about in your relationship.
- Encourages you.
- Knows how to keep a confidence.

Personal Competencies

Someone who:

- Has a thorough knowledge of the organization and its culture.
- Has a good understanding of the community.
- Possesses an area of expertise in which you are interested.
- Helps you reflect on your experiences as a volunteer and learn from them.
- Teaches you to be a mentor to other people.
- Serves as a motivational model for you.

You will want to have different kinds of mentors in different kinds of positions in the organization in which you are volunteering. Be pro-active in identifying and building relationships with members of the paid staff who can give you a range of perspectives about life in the organization. Building relationships with other volunteers can also be a great way to share experiences and to learn from each other. Having the opportunity to meet and get to know at least one member of the governing board of the organization in which you are volunteering can also be highly educational in helping you to have an overall view of the mission and work of the organization.

Don't underestimate the importance of having mentors in the process of maximizing the value of the volunteer experience. Time spent in finding, getting to know, and building relationships with mentors who are genuinely interested in your personal growth, development, and contribution, is time well spent. Building these relationships with mentors which will result in win-win relationships for them, for you, and for the organization, should be one of your top priorities as a volunteer.

Exhibit Trustworthy Behavior

In order to maximize the benefit from the volunteer experience, the volunteer needs to get his or her authority through actions and performance. This is because although volunteers may have a job description, their positions rarely appear on the organization chart. Lacking the legitimate authority that comes from a specific position on the organization chart, they must of necessity use their personal power to get the most out of the process of volunteering. At the core of their personal power is behaving in a trustworthy manner. As a volunteer it is necessary for you to establish your credibility through responsible behavior. You need to do what you say you will do. You need to be responsible, dependable, and honest in your actions. You need to earn the respect of those with whom you interact through your actions and your performance. This is of the essence in successfully doing your job, building relationships, and maximizing your learning opportunities. When a volunteer has earned the trust and respect of the other people in the organization, a wide range of opportunities open up for him or her that will add value to the volunteer experience.

Acting in a trustworthy manner opens up lines of communication with the people with whom the volunteer is interacting. Trusting relationships facilitate honest, accurate, and productive communication. Such communication is essential if the volunteer is to successfully meet his learning goals. Trustworthy behavior on the part of a volunteer, along with his or her non-threatening status, encourages other people in the organization to openly share information.

Acting in a trustworthy manner is important in developing and strengthening other attributes of good character. Honesty, fairness, integrity, loyalty, and compassion are all related to behaving in a trustworthy manner. Warren Bennis, a leading authority on leadership, states that "trust is the glue that holds organizations together." Being trustworthy also provides the foundation for maximizing the volunteer experience.

Utilize Your Creative Potential

In the previous chapter it was indicated that actions that can be taken to develop, use, and maximize your creative potential will be discussed in greater depth in this chapter. However, before discussing these action steps, let's talk briefly about why creativity is so important in the world today and about the nature of the creative process. Your volunteer experiences can be an important way to help you to develop your creativity and, in turn, this enhanced creativity can be used to maximize your experiences as a volunteer.

Utilizing your creativity has never been more important than it is in today's rapidly changing, fast-paced society. In the age of the knowledge worker, developing ideas that lead to creative solutions to the challenges facing us is of the first importance. In a society where most people use only a small percentage of their creative potential, it is imperative that this huge pool of creative energy be transformed into solution-solving initiatives. The effective utilization of our creative potential is essential for personal, organizational, and societal success. We cannot afford to waste this incredibly important resource.

Key to success in the creative process is the initial withholding of critical judgment. Many of us are trained to be "experts in criticism." When someone proposes a new idea, the "expert in criticism" begins immediately to think about what is wrong with it. This is often not only true of the person on the receiving end of the idea, but is also true of the person proposing the idea. The person proposing the idea says to himself: "This won't work — it's too radical, etc.," and eliminates an idea that has great potential. On the other end of the communication transaction, the receiver is thinking about what's wrong with the idea, rather than attempting to understand it.

Along with the withholding of judgment, the generation of large numbers of possible solutions to problems is also of the essence. The free-wheeling, non-judgmental development of large numbers of ideas is critical to creative solution finding. There is plenty of time in the next stage of the ideation process to critically review the ideas that are developed. Categorizing, prioritizing, and selecting the best ideas should only be done after large numbers of ideas are initially generated.

In the creative process, our objective is to come up with the best possible solutions to the challenges we face. This cannot be accomplished if possible solutions are prematurely eliminated before a full review of them can be made within a comprehensive framework of ideas.

The practice of premature judgment of ideas sets a tone that is highly detrimental to the creative process. Negativity rather than a positive outpouring of ideas sets a discouraging tone for the ongoing creative process. It becomes, in fact, an ongoing non-creative process.

With this brief introduction as a background to the creative process, let's talk now about action steps that you can take to maximize your creative potential, and in the process get more out of your volunteer experiences.

The not-for-profit organization provides an especially supportive environment in which to take these action steps because of its complexity, openness to volunteer involvement, commitment to employee participation, variety of committed mentors, involvement with partnerships and alliances, diversity of clients, dedication to mission, and the need to do more with fewer resources.

Action Steps to Increase and Utilize Your Creativity in the Volunteer Experience

✔ Locate an innovative organization.

✔ Associate with diverse groups of people.

✔ Identify and work with creative people.

✔ Associate with creative work groups.

✔ Learn from the overall environment.

✔ Keep the organizational philosophy, vision, and mission clearly in mind regarding desired outcomes.

✔ Learn from what other not-for-profit organizations are doing.

✔ Be aware of changes in the external environment.

✔ Learn from the culture and sub-cultures of the organization.

✔ Master the work you are doing in order to improve upon it.

✔ Be open to new ideas.

✔ Look for new and better ways of doing things.

✔ Experiment with new and different approaches.

✔ Withhold initial criticism.

✔ Develop and consider numbers of possible solutions to problems.

✔ Participate in brainstorming sessions.

✔ Look at issues from different perspectives.

✔ Solicit ideas for service improvements from clients.

✔ Solicit ideas for service improvements from co-workers.

One of the great things about volunteering is the opportunity to do things that you would not otherwise be able to do. In the process of volunteering it is important that you consider the potential that a particular organization has for enabling you to develop and use your creativity. It is also important that the organization in which you choose to volunteer encourages you to use your creativity in helping it accomplish its mission. Using your creativity to help

Wisdom from the
HAPPY VOLUNTEER

"Volunteering is a great way
to increase your self-confidence
and your sense of self-worth."

"Volunteering in not-for-profit
organizations provides you with greater
freedom to practice and exercise
your creativity because developing
creative solutions to improving
the human condition is what these
organizations are all about."

improve some aspect of the human condition will provide you with a real sense of satisfaction and joy. It can be, in fact, one of the great joys in life.

Learning from the Overall Organization

In order to get the most out of your volunteer experiences you should try to learn as much as you can from the overall organization. Make every effort to think about how the various aspects of the organization in which you are volunteering and its surrounding environment support and enrich your learning goals.

View your volunteer experiences as a "laboratory in learning." You have the opportunity to learn from the jobs attempted, the organization, the external environment, the clients who are served, the people who provide goods and services to the organization, and the communities which interact with the organization. This opportunity to learn about issues that are related to your learning goals could include areas of interest such as those indicated below under the heading, "The Enlightened Volunteer." You may wish to identify additional areas of potential interest to you to add to this list as you learn from the overall organization from your perspective as a volunteer.

The Enlightened Volunteer

The "enlightened volunteer" learns from the overall organization, and in the process focuses on aspects of organizational life, such as those listed in the following chart, that relate to his or her goals for the volunteer experience.

The Enlightened Volunteer

Organizational philosophy, vision, and mission	Power and influence
Organizational differentiation	Employee motivation
Leadership	Employee morale
Management	Cooperation & competition
Entrepreneurship	Interpersonal skills and competencies
Intrapreneurship	Networking
Decision-making	Alliances and partnerships
Risk taking	Trust and credibility
Strategic planning	Conflict resolution
Communication processes	Negotiation strategies
Organizational culture	Community building
The formal organizational structure	Marketing
The informal organizational structure	Customer service
Change processes	Delivery systems
Mentoring processes	Quality
Group processes	Production processes
Creativity and innovation	Teamwork

One of the best ways to learn about an overall organization and how it functions is to volunteer to serve on the governing board of a not-for-profit organization. These entities which operate under a variety of names such as board of directors, board of trustees, or board of governors, are responsible for formulating the policies which govern a not-for-profit organization. They also have the responsibility for the fiscal well-being of the organization and for selecting and supervising the chief executive officer. A unique function of not-for-profit organizations is that, in most cases, these governing bodies are comprised of unpaid volunteers.

Not-for-profit organizations are constantly looking for dedicated individuals to serve on their governing bodies. Look for an organization whose mission is important to you and check to see if there is an opportunity for you to serve on its governing body. In our discussions we will refer to the governing body as the board of directors since this is the term most commonly used by not-for-profit organizations.

Service as a volunteer on a board of directors of a not-for-profit organization provides you with a great opportunity for personal growth and enrichment. Such an experience is a wonderful way to help you to maximize the value of the volunteer experience. At the same time you will be providing a critically important service to the organization.

Service on the board of directors of a not-for-profit organization can provide you with the opportunity to:

- See the big picture — what the organization is all about and how it relates to the world around it (the external environment).

- Develop your conceptual skills — to visualize what is possible and ways in which the organizational vision and mission can be realized.
- Work with and learn from other talented volunteers.
- Be directly involved in creating the policies that drive the organization's actions.
- Observe the relationships between the various parts of the organization and how they work together to achieve desired outcomes.
- Be involved in the decision-making processes of the organization.
- Exercise your creativity at the highest organizational level.
- Be of service in a broad-based, significant manner.
- Provide input to the organization from the point of view of a member of the community in which the organization is located.
- Be involved doing important work that makes a difference.
- Develop your analytical skills.

Another good vantage point from which you may have the opportunity to view and learn from the overall organization is to serve on one of the organization's committees. Look for a committee that is of interest to you and that is of critical importance to the overall functioning of the organization. As you serve on this committee, try to learn as much as you can about the nature of its work, and how this work relates to the different parts of the organization, the environment in which it operates, and to its mission.

In the process of learning from the overall organization in which you are volunteering, try to identify the shared values, beliefs, norms, and assumptions that are present. These are of critical importance in creating the cultural framework within which the organization functions. Understanding the behavior of the people in an organization is dependent to a considerable degree upon understanding the culture and sub-cultures in which they live and work.

If you are to get the greatest value from your experiences as a volunteer, it is essential that you become aware of and appreciate the powerful impact of its culture and sub-cultures. In order to further your cultural understanding, make every effort to get to know diverse groups of people who are representative of a variety of sub-cultures within the organization in which you are volunteering. In addition, try to identify the shared values, beliefs, norms, and assumptions that are found in all of these sub-groups that tie together and unify the efforts of the organization to move forward to fulfill its mission. Gaining an understanding of the power and influence of organizational culture is one of the most important ways in which you can maximize your learning experiences as a volunteer.

As you observe the culture and sub-cultures of the organization in which you are volunteering, make a special effort to consider the following things:

- Degree of commitment to the organizational mission
- Acceptance and support of volunteers
- How leadership takes place
- How decisions are made
- Number of organizational levels
- Shared values, beliefs, norms, and assumptions
- Extent of employee participation in decision-making
- Degree of formality/informality

- Status symbols
- Extent to which it is a learning organization
- Characteristics of its work groups
- Organizational group cohesion
- Level of morale
- Level of trust
- Adaptability to change
- Degree of innovation
- Work area special arrangements
- Systems of recognition
- Organizational personality
- The way people dress

Learning about the culture and sub-cultures of the not-for-profit organization in which you are volunteering is one of the most fascinating aspects of the volunteer experience. It is a key component of learning from the overall organization. It should be an important part of your plan for realizing the maximum benefit from your volunteer experiences.

Participate in a Variety of Experiences

In your efforts as a volunteer to learn as much as possible from the overall organization, it is important that you identify and participate in a range of experiences that relate to your learning goals.

Participation provides insights into areas of organizational life that may not be evident to you if your role is limited to that of an observer. It is therefore important that you make every effort to become involved with a variety of experiences. Work this out in advance of beginning your volunteer experience if this is possible. Make it clear that you would like to have the opportunity to work on both a longer term project with which you could be involved from beginning to end, and also with a variety of projects that would allow you to have a more comprehensive understanding of the areas of work in which you are interested.

Participation makes possible both intellectual and emotional involvement with the work you are doing. Participation allows you, as a volunteer, to gain deeper insight into the work of the organization. Participation enables the individual to get a better feeling about his or her interest in a particular kind of work. The information is provided directly to the individual rather than through another person or through observation. Participation provides the volunteer with reality-based insight about specific jobs and different facets of organizational life.

Interact With and Learn from the Organization's Clients

The diverse clients of not-for-profit organizations provide a great learning opportunity for volunteers to develop their listening and mentoring skills.

Good listening skills are an essential part of being able to interact and communicate in authentic ways with other people. It is difficult if not impossible to help clients meet their needs without understanding the background that creates these needs. Volunteering provides the opportunity to practice listening to, and focusing on, client needs. Effective listening requires lots of practice in order to overcome the anti-listening behavior that many people have learned beginning with their childhood.

Wisdom from the
HAPPY VOLUNTEER

"Volunteer in order to discover
your passions in life."

"Volunteering is a great
way to help you develop
your spirituality."

Learning to be an effective listener can open up a new world of understanding for the volunteer. Listening with understanding will, in turn, provide the volunteer with the opportunity to be a solution finder and a mentor. Just as having mentors is of great value to the volunteer, so too is being a mentor to clients of the organization of great value to the volunteer. The mentoring process requires the one doing the mentoring to order one's thoughts, identify priorities, and develop and suggest alternative solutions. For this reason, in many cases, the mentor learns more from the process than the person being mentored. In turn, the clients of the organization who are helped by a volunteer can then become mentors to their friends who are in need of help.

One of the keys to helping clients achieve their goals and objectives is the development of trusting relationships. Trust is a critical ingredient of relationships that has been discussed previously in this book. Building such trust is at the heart of helping clients to be successful. The process of interacting directly with clients and helping them to succeed is one of the most satisfying experiences of being a volunteer.

Learn about Community Dynamics and Community Building

Volunteering in a not-for-profit organization provides an exceptional opportunity to learn about community dynamics and community building. This is because not-for-profit organizations operate in a wide range of areas that profoundly impact the manner in which communities function on a day-to-day basis. These areas of not-for-profit organization involvement in the community include, among others: the arts, athletics and recreation, business, education, environmental concerns, health-related issues, the political arena, religion and the spiritual life, and social service endeavors. Not-for-profit organizations relate to each of these areas through a broad spectrum of initiatives and activities. In Chapter 5, "Finding the Right Volunteer Opportunities in the Right Organizations," there is a more detailed discussion of each of these areas of not-for-profit organization involvement.

The special relationship of the not-for-profit organization to the community affords the volunteer with the opportunity to learn about such issues as envisioning the future, building agreed-upon action agendas, the development of community spirit, cooperation and conflict, political processes, the nature of community institutions, religious and ethnic groups, social class dynamics, and the development of community self-concept, among others.

One interesting way to observe and learn about the communities with which the not-for-profit organization in which you volunteer interacts is to examine them within the framework of Abraham Maslow's theory of the hierarchy of needs. Maslow's concept is that there is a triangle comprised of different levels of need. The lowest or base level of the triangle is comprised of physiological needs such as the need for food or water. The next higher level is comprised of safety needs, the next love and belongingness needs, the next esteem needs, and the highest, needs for self-actualization. Self-actualization involves the process of realizing your potential, of becoming what you are capable of becoming. According to Maslow's theory, when a level of need is largely satisfied then the next higher level of need is what will motivate an individual to take action. When a level of need is satisfied, then that level of need no longer serves as a motivator.

The author of this book had the experience of being involved in a planning process to determine, with input from the citizens of the community, what they wanted that city to be known for in the minds of the members of the general public. What was the first thing that the people involved in this process wanted other people to think of when the name of the city was mentioned? What was sought in the planning process were ideas about what the city wanted to be known for, what it wanted to become in order to achieve its greatest potential as a city. People from around the city were asked to provide written input into this process at a downtown office and to attend meetings to discuss their ideas.

Discussions at these meetings centered around items such as trash pick-up, garbage disposal, and police protection and public safety, which are at the bottom levels of Maslow's hierarchy of needs. The people in attendance at the public meetings weren't able to envision the issues at the desired higher level of self-actualization because they continued to be involved with lower level needs which had not been satisfied for them. It was the lower level, unsatisfied needs that continued to motivate them. This sort of behavior can be viewed first-hand by volunteers in not-for-profit organizations as they participate directly in the human improvement activities of the organization in which they are volunteering.

Involvement as a volunteer in a not-for-profit organization can also provide insights into a range of issues concerning how communities develop and achieve excellence. Among these issues are the development of a shared vision for the future along with shared beliefs, values, and expectations. The process by which community pride and a sense of civic responsibility develop can also be observed first-hand.

These are all elements of the self-concept of a community which influence its goals and its behavior. Communities which perceive themselves as being capable of doing first-rate things are usually far more successful than communities which perceive themselves as being second or third rate. It is difficult to achieve first-rate results if you perceive yourself as third-rate.

Being a Happy Volunteer

Questions to ask yourself after reading this chapter:

How can I clarify my goals for the volunteer experience?

What can I do to achieve mutually agreed-upon goals concerning my performance as a volunteer?

How can I best be pro-active in participating in a variety of experiences and in learning from the overall organization?

How can I build upon my special status as a volunteer to maximize the personal enrichment benefits of the volunteer experience?

How can I get feedback concerning whether or not I am behaving in a trustworthy manner in my role as a volunteer?

How can I best interact with and learn from the clients of the organization in which I am volunteering?

What actions can I take to learn about community dynamics and community building?

Chapter 3 — Using Volunteer Experiences to Advance Your Career

Volunteering in not-for-profit organizations can greatly assist you in advancing your career in paid positions. This is because volunteering can provide you with the opportunity to:

- Get the kind of experiences you need when you need them.
- Select volunteer experiences that allow you to build on and refine your strengths.
- Experience first-hand the nature and power of non-financial motivators.
- Develop your "personal power."
- Experience greater freedom in exercising your creativity.
- Expand your network of mentors and other resource people.
- Observe and become involved with the technological/human condition interface.

In pursuing these opportunities, be certain to build upon your special attributes as a volunteer. As we have discussed previously, these include your demonstrated commitment by working without monetary compensation, your non-threatening status, the fact that you are helping rather than competing, the interest that others have in your motivation to contribute, and the desire of people in the organization to help you achieve your personal goals, since that is the compensation that you are receiving for your work in helping to achieve the organizational mission.

The following pages discuss opportunities available to you as a volunteer to assist you in your career success. Clear goals are essential if you are to use these opportunities to learn from the overall organization. Careful research, planning, prioritizing, and good time management are important in the process of identifying, selecting, and participating in the volunteer opportunities which will best assist you in moving ahead in your career.

Opportunities Available through Volunteering to Help You Advance Your Career

Opportunity No. 1 — Get the Kind of Experiences You Need When You Need Them

We mentioned earlier in this book that volunteering in not-for-profit organizations can provide you, as a volunteer, with experiences that are relevant to your needs at a particular time in your life. This is equally true of career competencies that are required at specific points in time. This is possible because of the wide range of opportunities available at many different locations. It may also be possible to access many of these opportunities to develop career competencies through the use of present and emerging technologies which provide instant time and place utility. Utility is the ability to satisfy your needs and wants by providing the desired experiences at times and places that are readily accessible to you. The nine different areas of endeavor for improving the human condition mentioned in the introduction to this book provide the depth, diversity, and richness of career enhancement opportunities appropriate to different stages of your career development.

Key to utilizing the richness of your career advancement opportunities through volunteering is the fact that you are in the driver's seat in finding and participating in the experiences you are looking for, rather than being dependent upon some outside entity to do the choosing for you. Since volunteers are always in demand in not-for-profit organizations, you have the ability to choose which opportunities you will pursue and how long you will pursue them. You can tailor your career development opportunities to meet your specific needs when you most need them.

In addition, another great advantage to developing career competencies as a volunteer is that you are doing this outside of your regular career activities. You are not being limited and constrained by the parameters of your principal job. You have greater freedom to try new things and to experiment with innovative ways of doing things that might not be possible for you to do in your regular job. Volunteer positions are frequently less rigidly defined, which allows more freedom of action.

When volunteering, you want to build into your initial agreement with the organization in which you are volunteering the ability to volunteer in different functional areas of the organization. This will permit you to better meet your needs to acquire the experiences that you most need at a particular point in time in your career. If the organization in which you are volunteering is involved with different areas or fields of human improvement activity, you should choose several areas of activity most appropriate to

Wisdom from the
HAPPY VOLUNTEER

"Volunteering in not-for-profit organizations provides relevant and timely career development experiences at no risk to your present job."

"You have the ability to select and shape the nature of your experiences as a volunteer in ways that will best assist your career development and future success."

your present career development needs. This will give you greater flexibility in meeting your needs in a timely manner.

Volunteering in not-for-profit organizations provides relevant and timely career development experiences at no risk to your career advancement with your present employer. Not only are you able to participate in experiences not available to you with your present employer, but you are able to get these experiences without taking risks with your present career. In addition, the fact that you are volunteering in other organizational settings than that of your paid position provides you with the opportunity to gain insight into new and different career possibilities and organizational cultures. This is especially valuable if you are in the process of re-examining where you presently are in your career and are thinking about heading off in new directions. Volunteering provides the vehicle for gaining needed insights to successfully move forward with this process in an efficient and effective manner. Remember, you have the ability to select and shape the nature of your experiences as a volunteer in ways that will best assist your career development and future success.

Volunteering in not-for-profit organizations offers you the opportunity to tap into the network that enables these organizations to successfully achieve their missions. Tapping into these networks provides another great way to get the kinds of career development experiences you need when you need them. These networks are comprised of suppliers, clients, community organizations, the public sector, the private sector, other not-for-profit organizations, communities served by the organization and others who interact with the organization in which you are volunteering. Access to these networking groups and individuals offer the volunteer a broad range of opportunities for getting relevant career-related competencies in a timely and efficient manner. These opportunities will be discussed in more depth later in this chapter.

Opportunity No. 2 — Select Volunteer Experiences that Allow You to Build On and Refine Your Strengths

In order to build a successful career it is important to identify, build on, refine, and utilize your personal strengths. Volunteering in not-for-profit organizations can be of great assistance in this process because these organizations are in the human improvement business. As you work to help others develop their personal strengths and realize their potential, there is a great opportunity for you to utilize and build upon your own strengths.

The concept of utilizing and building upon the things you are good at is a key to your career advancement. If you are to stand out from the pack, it is essential that you develop the strengths that make you a unique, important, contributing member of society. Far too many people spend far too much time working on their deficiencies rather than working on their strengths.

Building upon the things that you do best is the way in which you achieve excellent performance and make a maximum contribution to yourself and the organization in which you work. This is also the way in which you receive the greatest satisfaction in your work. Being a volunteer in a not-for-profit human improvement organization allows you to practice and refine the skills and competencies that make you a unique and important contributor.

Knowing what you do best allows you, as you advance in management and leadership positions, to enlist the efforts of people whose skills and competencies complement your own and those of the other members of your team. A frequent obstacle to career advancement is the tendency of many people to employ individuals who possess the same strengths as their own. There is a fear that hiring someone who knows more about some area than you do will place you in a dependent position. This is often a self-confidence issue that needs to be overcome in order to build really effective teams.

Use volunteer experiences to get feedback about how others perceive your skills and competencies. Volunteering in not-for-profit organizations affords you the opportunity to get feedback from your supervisor, other employees, other volunteers, clients, suppliers, and members of the community. Make a special effort to get feedback concerning how you and your performance are perceived by these individuals and groups.

Opportunity No. 3 — Examine First-hand the Nature and Power of Non-financial Motivators

Sustained excellent performance is a key ingredient in advancing your career. There are quite a few people who perform well for short periods of time but are unable to sustain their level of performance over the longer term. It is the author's belief that, in many cases, a lack of non-financial motivators is responsible for this drop off in performance. Careers in sales are an excellent case in point. It is a common thing for individuals to go into sales because they feel that they can make a great deal of money doing it. Their motivation is simply to make money and they lack other reasons for wanting to sell, such as providing a valuable needed service or improving the quality of life of the recipient. Their sole purpose in selling is to make money for themselves. Before long many of these individuals "burn out." They come to strongly dislike what they are doing and get tired of faking an interest in selling. There are inadequate non-financial motivators to give them the personal satisfaction that they require to continue functioning in sales with excellence. They have no interest in sustaining what is a meaningless endeavor for them. They don't believe that they are performing a societal function that has any value.

It seems apparent that non-financial motivators such as recognition, personal satisfaction, sense of meaning, sense of contribution, and self-actualization are essential to sustained excellent performance. The process of volunteering demonstrates to the individuals involved in a very personal way the power of non-financial motivators.

Volunteers are not receiving financial compensation but are giving their time, effort, energy, and commitment to causes and endeavors in which they believe. They are experiencing in a first-hand way the importance of the personal rewards that they receive from being volunteers. The importance of non-financial motivators is underscored. They come to more fully realize that in their regular paid employment these non-financial motivators play an important part in the performance of employees, along with the financial compensation they receive. They realize that money is only a part of the motivational dimension of these employees and that it alone is inadequate to support sustained excellent performance.

It is common for non-financial motivators to be given inadequate attention by managers and leaders in business and professional organizations. Volunteering in various settings in not-for-profit organizations gives the volunteer the understanding and insight that facilitates the more effective utilization of these motivators in his or her career in other organizational settings.

Opportunity No. 4 — Developing Your "Personal Power"

Your "personal power" is comprised of the personal resources that you can bring to bear on the actions you chose to take. Using your personal power involves tapping into your inner resources in order to achieve goals that are important to you. This involves the confidence and courage to take action and to stay the course.

Using your personal power involves believing in yourself and your abilities and persevering in your efforts to successfully achieve desired outcomes. You believe that you can make things happen; that most things are under your control. You are pro-active in bringing about desired changes and desired actions. You believe that you have the ability to plan and implement change. You do not believe that you are a victim of change who is completely at the mercy of the environment in which you live. You believe that to a considerable extent you can determine your own destiny. You believe you have within you the resources to live a worthwhile, productive, and satisfying life. You have the confidence that you can stand on your own two feet and that you can live a productive, fulfilling, and happy life with the resources available to you.

The volunteer experience can be highly supportive in helping to develop your personal power. This is because, in an environment that values and supports the work of volunteers, there is often the opportunity for volunteers to become involved in the process of defining their roles. Many volunteer roles are not defined in a detailed way and, as noted previously, are not specifically identified on the organization chart. This usually allows for some room for these roles to evolve and develop with the performance of the individual volunteer. In short, you, as a volunteer, are to some extent on your own. You are called upon to develop your role as a volunteer. You are frequently on your own to a greater extent than in a paid position. You are more dependent on your personal power in achieving success. This necessity to develop your own credibility as a contributor to the organization enables you, as a volunteer, to practice and strengthen the attributes that increase your ability to function effectively.

In order to be successful as a volunteer, you learn that it is essential for you to develop excellent listening skills. This is of critical importance in helping to identify and meet the needs of the other volunteers and the paid staff with whom you are working, as well as the clients being served. Being a volunteer is a great way to come to understand the "enlightened self-interest" that motivates the people with whom you are working to take the actions that they do and behave in certain ways. The volunteer process forces the volunteer to become a good listener because it is only through listening and responding to what is learned that a volunteer is able to take the actions that are necessary to gain the needed credibility to influence the behaviors of other people.

In order to advance your career in paid positions, you must have the confidence, courage, and perseverance to stay the course to achieve your goals. Increasingly, employees in the workforce are called upon to function as entrepreneurs within the organization in which they work. In an increasingly project-based work environment, the ability to utilize the full scope of one's personal resources in the accomplishment of organizational goals is of the utmost importance. Being a volunteer is great training for developing the entrepreneurial instinct whether it is used in starting and operating one's own business or in working in other organizational settings. Developing one's personal power — one's ability to utilize one's personal resources in the pursuit of desired outcomes — is of the essence for career advancement in a highly competitive, rapidly changing work environment.

Opportunity No. 5 — Experience Greater Freedom in Exercising Your Creativity

Creativity has never been more important than in today's highly competitive, rapidly changing world. In order to move your career ahead you have to deal creatively with this "new world" in which we live.

Volunteering in not-for-profit organizations provides you with greater freedom to practice and exercise your creativity because developing creative solutions to improving the human condition is what these organizations are all about. The fact that not-for-profit organizations are mission-driven rather than profit-driven provides an environment in which new and different initiatives can be undertaken with less regard to making a profit. "Bottom line thinking" sometimes eliminates creative possibilities because the financial risk is considered to be too great.

Not-for-profit organizations are frequently called upon to perform societal functions that public sector and private sector organizations are unable to do, or do not want to do because of other goals, objectives, and constraints placed upon them. Not-for-profits are therefore required to utilize their creativity as the foundation of the way in which they operate. They are expected to be creative. They

Wisdom from the
HAPPY VOLUNTEER

"One of the great things about
being a volunteer is that you are
able to make choices concerning
what you want to do and
where you want to do it."

"Volunteering encourages you to be
pro-active, self-motivated, self-reliant,
and to be a self-directed learner."

have a public trust to be creative. They have the freedom to be creative.

Volunteering in an organization that has a culture of creativity permits the volunteer to both observe and participate in the creative process in a highly reality-centered environment. There is no more reality-centered environment than one in which the work involves improving the human condition.

One of the major components of being in the human improvement business is working to increase the self-esteem of the individuals involved in the process. This is of the essence in taking advantage of the greater freedom to develop and implement creative solutions in not-for-profit organizations. In order to participate effectively in the creative process you, as a volunteer, have to believe that you have the personal resources to deal with the challenges facing you. You have to have the self-confidence to be pro-active in pursuing needed solutions. It takes courage to be creative and try new approaches. It takes courage to believe in yourself and your capabilities. Volunteering in not-for-profit organizations can provide you with an environment that encourages you to value your capabilities and to become creatively involved in the process of helping to find solutions to challenging problems.

One of the important lessons that the author of this book learned in his experiences in working with managers at different organizational levels is that in many cases the individuals who rose to higher levels in the organization attempted solution strategies and actions that other individuals who were less successful believed were closed to them. They perceived as impossible actions that those who were more successful chose to take. The more successful managers had the courage to utilize their creativity in doing what others perceived as impossible. Volunteering in creatively functioning not-for-profit organizations can help you to broaden your perspective concerning possible solutions that are available in the problem-solving process.

Opportunity No. 6 — Expand Your Network of Mentors and Other Resource People

In this book we have talked about volunteering in not-for-profit organizations as a great way to get to know people who can introduce you to exciting new opportunities for your personal growth and development as you work to help others.

Some of these resource people that you meet and get to know in your experiences as a volunteer will most likely become friends as well as resource people who you will want to keep in touch with over the years. Some may become mentors to you in areas of career interest to you. Some, in fact, may be mentors, advisors, and important resource people in helping you to achieve career goals in areas of future employment.

The role of mentors, people who take a special interest in you, can be of great importance in your personal development and future career success. Volunteering enables you to seek out, get to know, and work with individuals you might not have the opportunity to meet in your regular job. In addition, the fact that you are a volunteer working without financial compensation, who is interested in learning new things and gaining new experiences while helping others, allows for an especially productive and worthwhile relationship with resource people and potential mentors. These individuals realize that your compensation for volunteering is the value and outcome of the volunteer work you are doing and the new insights, competencies, and other personal enrichment benefits that you receive. This knowledge is frequently a motivation driving them to assist in your personal learning process.

While resource people in not-for-profit organizations possess many of the same characteristics as resource people in private sector organizations, their focus is on achieving the mission of the organization in which they work. Their concern is not to generate income for stockholders as is the case in for-profit organizations. Achieving the organizational mission of improving some aspect of the human condition is the sole purpose of the not-for-profit organization. This emphasis on achieving the organizational mission, the purpose of the organization, teaches the volunteer to focus on the importance of factors in organizational life in addition to the "bottom line."

In an age of incredibly rapid change it is critically important for an individual to be able to identify and access needed resources quickly for career success. The individual who has a network of resource people and mentors in place is in an excellent position to achieve superior results. Volunteering in not-for-profit organizations is a wonderful way to expand this network in a range of areas related to your career goals. In choosing organizations in which to volunteer, consider carefully the availability of resource people and potential mentors relevant to your learning and career goals. Look first for organizations with a mission in which you are deeply interested and can be strongly committed to and then examine carefully the nature of the potential resource people and mentors who are involved with the work of the organization.

Opportunity No. 7 — Observe and Become Involved with the Technological/Human Condition Interface

One of the most important things that you can do to advance your career is to help yourself and those with whom you work develop and utilize potential ability. A major issue in organizational life is getting the people involved to do what they are capable of doing. Wouldn't it be a wonderful thing if we could get people to utilize eighty percent of their intellectual and creative power, rather than twenty or twenty-five percent, in the pursuit of organizational goals and objectives? How does one get people turned on and excited about the work they are performing?

In an age where the use of all kinds of technology is expanding at a rapid rate, knowing how to use this technology in ways that encourage the utilization of human potential is all important. Volunteering in not-for-profit organizations provides the volunteer with first-hand experience in observing and being involved with the technological/human condition interface. This is because not-for-profit organizations are frequently faced with a large demand for their services and fewer traditional resources to get the job done. This forces them to utilize technology in solving the specific problems which they face in improving the human condition in their particular areas of expertise. One of the advantages of using technology in the development of humane and motivating systems is that more people can be reached and helped.

It is important to remember that the common concern of all not-for-profit organizations is the fact that they are in the human improvement business. What a great opportunity for the volunteer to observe, study, and become involved with the technological/human condition interface. The fact that not-for-profit organizations have a special responsibility and public trust to serve as models in the development of technologically humane systems that prove that technology can be supportive in improving the human condition underscores the importance of this learning environment.

The insights which you gain as a volunteer in observing first-hand the technological/human condition interaction, are directly applicable to your development as a manager and leader in paid positions. You will have had the opportunity to experience first-hand the energy, excitement, and outstanding performance that is possible when serious attention is given to the proper and creative use of technology and the value inherent in the human beings who use this technology.

Being a Happy Volunteer

Questions to ask yourself after reading this chapter:

- What are the personal development experiences that I need most at this particular time in my life to advance my career?

- What are my personal strengths that I want to further strengthen and develop?

- How can I use my personal strengths to help the organization in which I am volunteering move forward in achieving its mission?

- What have I learned about the importance and power of motivators other than money?

- How can I use my knowledge of the importance and power of non-financial motivators to motivate myself and others in my regular job?

- What have I learned in this chapter about self-reliance and self-initiative that will be useful in advancing my career?

- How can I have volunteer experiences that will allow me to exercise greater creativity?

- How can I best identify the mentors and resource people who will be most helpful in my career development?

- How can I best get an overall view of the organization that will enable me to observe the impact of technology on the morale, personal satisfaction, happiness, and productivity of its people?

Chapter 4 —
Achieving Life Goals
through Volunteering

Volunteering in not-for-profit organizations is a great way to help you identify and work toward the realization of life goals. Life goals are those goals that are of central importance to you as you live your life. These are the goals that give your life its sense of purpose and meaning. Life goals serve as strong motivators for you in determining what is of the first importance to you and how you choose to live your life.

Following is a listing of examples of life goals. As you read over this list, which of these goals resonates with you? Are any of these goals of the first importance to you? At this point in your life what goals would you add or delete from the list?

Examples of Life Goals

❑ Discovering who you are in order to realize your potential.

❑ Using your potential to be of service to other people.

❑ Having a sense of personal worth, being happy, and helping other people to be happy.

❑ Loving and being loved in a family relationship and contributing to this relationship.

❑ Taking charge of your life.

Wisdom from the
HAPPY VOLUNTEER

"Through insights gained in the
reality-centered not-for-profit organization,
the volunteer is better able to determine
the relative importance of life goals."

"Discovering which goals are of
central importance to you as you live
your life and acting to achieve them
is of critical importance in living a
purposeful and fulfilling life."

❏ Developing a rich spiritual life.

❏ Having a productive and rewarding work life.

❏ Developing character strengths that enable you to realize your potential and contribute to others.

❏ Developing an appreciation for the human condition and having compassion for yourself and other people.

❏ Appreciating and honoring the uniqueness of each human being.

❏ Having good friends with whom you can have a trusting relationship and with whom you can share life experiences.

The process of volunteering in not-for-profit organizations can be of great help to you in formulating and implementing your own life goals for the following reasons:

• Not-for-profit organizations are in the business of helping people achieve life goals.

• There is a wide choice of volunteer opportunities and experiences available to you.

• You are in the driver's seat in determining the nature and duration of the experiences for which you are volunteering.

Potential Areas of Not-for-Profit Volunteer Involvement

As mentioned previously in this book, not-for-profit organizations are involved with a wide spectrum of fields of endeavor. Among these are: the arts, social service, the environment, political, health-related, business, education, religious/spiritual, and athletics/recreation. The following chart shows how these potential areas of not-for-profit volunteer involvement can be related to life goals.

Related Life Goals	Areas of Not-for-Profit Volunteer Involvement
Creating and appreciating beauty in the world.	The Arts
Being of service to other people.	Social Service
Having a productive and satisfying work life.	Business
Caring for the environment in which we live.	The Environment
Sustaining physical and mental well-being.	Athletics/ Recreation
Having a sense of purpose and meaning in life beyond that of material well-being.	Religious/Spiritual
Being a responsible citizen and participating in the political process.	Political
Being a continuing learner.	Education
Encouraging and supporting physical and mental well-being.	Health-Related

Following are brief descriptions of some of the kinds of volunteer opportunities available in different areas of volunteer involvement in not-for-profit organizations. As you look at these descriptions of possible opportunities, try to identify the ones which will best assist you at the present time in achieving your short-term and long-term life goals. In the process of identifying helpful volunteer experiences, think about how these experiences can be planned to build upon each other in order to best achieve these life goals.

The Arts

Not-for-profit arts organizations of all kinds offer wonderful opportunities for rich, rewarding volunteer experiences. These opportunities may be found in art museums, theatre groups, art associations, literary societies, writers' groups, orchestras, glee clubs and choral societies, opera houses, and arts programming on radio, television, and the internet. They may also be found in painters' groups, sculptors' groups, musical societies, drama societies, organizations involved with ballet and other forms of dance, and cultural societies of all kinds.

Not-for-profit arts organizations play a critically important role in transmitting the culture from one generation to the next. They also play an important role in encouraging the creative experimentation and innovation in the arts that opens up new worlds of understanding, appreciation, thought, and beauty for people of all ages.

Volunteering in not-for-profit arts organizations provides the opportunity for the volunteer to be part of this exciting and energizing process. Here again we have a win-win situation. The volunteer enriches his or her life and, in turn, enriches the life of the organization in which the volunteering takes place.

It is interesting to note that there are frequently many more volunteers in not-for-profit arts organizations than there are paid employees. This fact underscores the importance of the volunteer contribution. The volunteer is not just a volunteer, but a critical component of the organization's success.

Athletics/Recreation

There is a wide array of not-for-profit organizations that are involved with the support and ongoing operation of athletic and recreational programs. Participating as a volunteer in some aspect of these programs can be personally exciting, enriching, fulfilling, and growth-producing for a volunteer.

Emphasis in these programs is frequently centered on such issues as improved mental and physical health, the pursuit of excellence, sportsmanship, cooperation and competition, and the importance of persistence and practice in improving performance. Recreational programs of various kinds are also intended to provide relaxation, fun, and enjoyment.

Examples of not-for-profit organizations operating in the athletic and recreational area are: foundations supporting athletic participation, athletic and recreational leagues of all kinds, athletic alumni associations, park and recreational facilities, museums focusing on specific sports, hall of fame organizations, organizations for athletic coaches, organizations for sports officials, recreational and sports programs, and facilities operated by churches, the YMCA, the YWCA, Boys and Girls Clubs, schools, colleges, and universities, professional organizations which serve as governing bodies for specific sports such as baseball, tennis, football, basketball, soccer, etc., broad-based governing bodies which supervise multiple sports such as the NCAA, and a wide variety of clubs such as athletic clubs, sailing clubs, hiking clubs, travel clubs, fishing clubs, and sports car clubs.

Business

There are a large number of not-for-profit organizations that deal with some aspect of the role and function of business and the business community in the broader society. These organizations include, among others: local and state chambers of commerce, the United States Chamber of Commerce, small business associations, special interest business groups, trade associations, business groups representing specific professions, business clubs, entrepreneurial clubs, free enterprise clubs and associations, management clubs, leadership clubs, management training and professional development organizations and groups, publishing groups, specialized broad-based business groups such as those for business and professional women, institutes, think tanks, and foundations which focus on business issues and concerns.

These not-for-profit organizations make available to the volunteer a highly productive environment for personal enrichment, growth, and contribution. As in other areas of volunteer involvement, the volunteer is able to make choices about the volunteer experience. The volunteer is the key decision-maker concerning the nature and duration of his or her involvement in the volunteer experience.

Education

Educational institutions of all kinds provide a wide range of opportunities for volunteers. These opportunities are found in pre-schools, kindergartens, elementary schools, middle schools, high schools, colleges, and universities. Adult education institutions and programs also provide fertile ground for the involvement of volunteers. Non-traditional educational organizations offer numerous opportunities for volunteers. Many of these educational institutions and programs are not-for-profit organizations.

Educational institutions have a responsibility to foster the ongoing process of inquiry and self-directed learning. Individuals who volunteer in educational institutions should benefit from being part of this culture of self-inquiry and self-directed learning by integrating these values into their own learning strategies and practices.

Volunteering in educational institutions should encourage the volunteer to be a continuing learner who explores new possibilities for personal growth and contribution. The world view of the volunteer should be expanded in the volunteer process.

The Environment

Volunteering to work with not-for-profit environmental groups can be an incredibly enriching experience. You, as a volunteer, will have the opportunity to help preserve and safeguard the environment in which we live; to be part of the army of volunteers who work each day to help to preserve the beauty and magnificence of our natural world.

As with other fields with which not-for-profit organizations are involved, as a volunteer, you have many choices concerning how you will become involved in our society's efforts to preserve and safeguard our external environment.

Areas for possible volunteer involvement are: Audubon societies at the local, state, and national level, nature conservancies, wildlife federations, wilderness societies, wildlife sanctuaries, land preservation societies, forest preservation groups, animal protection groups, marine societies, professional groups dealing with the protection and preservation of specific types and categories of wildlife, historic areas and parks, horticultural societies, garden clubs, botanical groups and societies, animal preservation groups, and foundations which support conservation and land acquisition efforts.

Health-Related

Health-related organizations provide many opportunities for personal growth and enrichment through the volunteer experience. As with other fields of volunteer involvement, many of these experiences can be used to advance your career as a paid employee, if that is one of your personal goals.

Volunteer opportunities are frequently available in not-for-profit health-related organizations such as hospitals, mental health facilities of all kinds, rehabilitation centers, home health agencies, assisted living facilities, nursing homes, wellness centers, hospice houses, sports medicine clinics, athletic clubs, and many other specialized health care facilities.

The volunteer experience in health-related institutions is frequently an especially rich and rewarding one for volunteers because their efforts are deeply appreciated by the clients who are being served. This is because these clients are often experiencing a great deal of personal stress.

Health-related not-for-profit organizations offer an exceptionally wide range of choices and settings for volunteer involvement. As you consider settings for the realization of your life goals through volunteering, be sure to give careful attention to not-for-profit organizations in health-related fields.

Political

The political arena offers many opportunities for volunteer participation on the local, state, national, and international level. There are many opportunities to be directly involved in the political organizations of individuals running for political office. In addition, special interest organizations of all kinds are interested in involving volunteers in their efforts. So too are organizations created to encourage good government and responsible citizen involvement. Many of these groups and organizations are not-for-profits. They offer the volunteer excellent opportunities for personal growth and enrichment.

Volunteering in the political arena is a wonderful way in which to develop one's understanding of societal values and issues and to develop a deeper and broader perspective concerning one's responsibilities as a citizen.

Social Service

Not-for-profit social service organizations are concerned with the welfare of people who are dealing with such problems as alienation and isolation, inadequate housing, homelessness, lack of food, low income, and lack of adequate clothing. These organizations will sometimes develop partnerships and alliances with other not-for-profit organizations whose primary focus is education, health, legislative reform, or some other area of common concern. Participation with a not-for-profit social service organization involved with such cooperative ventures can be especially rewarding and enriching for the volunteers who are involved.

Examples of social service not-for-profit organizations are senior citizen centers and senior citizen transportation agencies, organizations for retired people, shelters for the homeless, food pantries, clothing programs for the needy, anti-poverty programs of various kinds, disaster relief agencies, youth-serving organizations such as Boys and Girls Clubs, the Girl Scouts, the Boy Scouts, Habitat for Humanity, the Salvation Army, Alcoholics Anonymous, and social service clubs which support community social needs such as Rotary, Lions, Kiwanis, Exchange Club, Soroptimists, and business and professional women's clubs.

Social service organizations provide the volunteer with a wide range of choices for volunteer involvement. Volunteer efforts are especially rewarding in social service not-for-profit organizations because of the importance of the work for both the organization and for the clients who are being served. Many of these critically important institutions could not continue to exist without the participation of volunteers.

Religious/Spiritual

There is more volunteer involvement in religious institutions than anywhere else. Opportunities abound for meaningful and important volunteer involvement. It is important to note that the great majority of individuals

Wisdom from the
HAPPY VOLUNTEER

"Volunteering in not-for-profit organizations is a great way to help you identify and work toward the realization of life goals."

"The process of life goal identification and realization can work either way; you can begin with short-term life goals that eventually transition into long-term life goals, or you can begin with long-term life goals and then proceed to identify and realize short-term life goals that will allow you to achieve your long-term life goals. This is the "circular process of life goal development and achievement.""

who participate in the life of religious institutions are volunteers.

Areas for volunteer involvement include a wide spectrum of responsibilities. Some of these are: membership on a board of trustees, being a deacon, participating in youth, adult, and secondary school programs, participating in the administration of church offices, and serving on church organizations and committees. Examples of these church organizations and committees might include the following: The Church Guild, membership, investment, hospitality, music, buildings and grounds, community outreach, public relations and publicity, visitation, and fundraising.

Volunteer participation in the life of religious institutions opens up a wonderful world of service and meaning for the individuals involved. Emphasis is upon discovering what is of first importance in living one's life and upon values and beliefs that transcend the material dimensions of our contemporary culture.

Volunteer participation in religious institutions provides the opportunity to develop and build strength of character, belief, faith and service. The work involved is of the greatest importance and the sense of fulfillment and contribution can be incredibly rewarding for the individuals who are involved. You are encouraged to explore volunteer opportunities involving spiritual growth and development as part of the planning process for your volunteer experiences.

～

The nine major areas of focus of not-for-profit organizations which have just been discussed provide an outstanding opportunity for volunteers to identify, work on, and achieve personal life goals; those goals that are of central importance to you as you live your life. The number and diversity of volunteer opportunities available in not-for-profit organizations enables the volunteer to actively participate in what we will call the "circular process of life goal development and achievement."

Some volunteers may begin this process by having certain long-term goals such as were mentioned earlier in this chapter. For example, a long-term life goal might be developing character strengths that will enable you to realize your potential and use it to contribute to others. The volunteer who begins with this long-term life goal in mind may decide to volunteer in a social service not-for-profit organization that deals with individuals who feel isolated and alienated from the broader society. The short-term life goal of the volunteer is to learn how to build trusting relationships with clients served by this organization. The volunteer develops the character strengths of honesty and integrity in the process of building trusting relationships. The next step is to identify and participate in additional short-term life goal experiences that will result in achieving the long-term life goal of developing one's character strengths, realizing and utilizing one's potential, and increasing one's contribution to others.

Conversely, another volunteer may begin the volunteer process with short-term life goals; goals that are of central importance to him or her at that particular time in his or her life, and out of these short-term life goals may emerge overriding long-term life goals.

The process of life goal identification and realization can work either way; you can begin with short-term life goals that eventually transition into long-term life goals, or you can begin with long-term life goals and then proceed to identify and realize short-term life goals that will allow you to achieve your long-term life goals. This is the "circular process of life goal development and achievement."

The volunteer process allows the volunteer to actively work on specific projects that will enable him or her to think about short-term or long-term life goals in clearer and more concrete ways. Through insights gained in the reality-centered, not-for-profit organization, the volunteer is better able to determine the relative importance of life goals. The volunteer is an active participant rather than merely an observer in this process of identifying and then working toward the realization of life goals.

Making life goals clear and more concrete greatly assists the volunteer in determining which goals are of first importance. Clear and concrete life goals are far more motivating than goals which are vague and ill-defined. In addition, clarity of life goals is important in sustaining progress toward the attainment of these goals over an extended period of time.

Discovering which goals are of central importance to you as you live your life, and acting to achieve them, is of critical importance in living a purposeful and fulfilling life. A major reason that the "Happy Volunteer" is happy is that he or she has identified life goals through the volunteer experience that are personally relevant and in keeping with his or her authentic self.

The author of this book encourages you to become a "Happy Volunteer" by discovering and pursuing important and personally rewarding life goals through the volunteer experience.

Being a Happy Volunteer

Questions to ask yourself after reading this chapter:

- At this point in my life what are my short-term and long-term life goals?

- Will achieving my present short-term life goals lead me toward the realization of my long-term life goals?

- In which of the nine areas of involvement of not-for-profit organizations am I most interested in volunteering at the present time?

- What resource people can I talk to who can help me to review, think about, clarify, and prioritize my short-term and long-term goals?

- What are the specific kinds of experiences I would like to have at this time that are related to my life goals?

Chapter 5 — Finding the Right Volunteer Opportunities in the Right Organizations

In this book we have talked about the many personal enrichment benefits of being a volunteer. We have also discussed ways in which you, as a volunteer, can receive the greatest value from your volunteer experiences by maximizing these benefits. In addition, we have discussed in some depth how you can achieve career and life goals through your volunteer experiences. In this Chapter our discussion focuses on how you can find the volunteer opportunities you are looking for in a not-for-profit organization that will support and appreciate your personal enrichment, career, and life goals. It is important that you take the time to find a not-for-profit organization that will be a good match for you in helping you to experience the joy, satisfaction, and sense of personal meaning and accomplishment that you are looking for in the volunteer process. An organization whose mission is important, exciting, and personally rewarding to you. Volunteering in an organization that you have little personal feeling for is not likely to meet your goals.

The process of finding exciting, important, and meaningful volunteer experiences does not have to be complex and time consuming. Following the suggestions in this chapter should enable you to find the kinds of volunteer

Wisdom from the
HAPPY VOLUNTEER

"Prior to developing a list of specific
not-for-profit organizations that you believe
can provide you, as a volunteer, with the best
environment to reach your goals, it is important
that you carefully consider your values and
preferences concerning the work environment."

"An organization's attitude concerning
the importance of volunteers in helping to
achieve its mission should be of central
importance in your decision concerning the
place where you want to volunteer."

opportunities you are looking for in an organization that is interested in supporting your efforts to achieve your goals, as you help it to achieve its mission.

Central to this process is the question regarding whether the organization in which you are thinking about volunteering considers volunteers to be full-fledged members of the staff who are valuable contributors in helping it to achieve its mission. Are volunteers perceived as important contributors to the success of the organization?

You may become involved as a volunteer in a specific organization in a variety of ways. For example, you may have a friend suffering from some kind of physical disability who is currently residing in a health care center of some kind. You decide to volunteer at that particular health care center because your friend is there and you want to be of service to him. In another case, you may be asked to become a volunteer member of the board of directors of a not-for-profit historical society because of your expertise in a specific area of local history. In another case, your employer may encourage you to volunteer in a certain not-for-profit organization with which the organization in which you work has developed some cooperative ventures. These are examples of situations in which you have not been required to do a comparative analysis of possible volunteer opportunities.

The action steps discussed below are suggested when you are attempting to achieve certain personal goals in the volunteer experience and need to examine different opportunities in different organizations. You are doing this in the effort to best meet your learning goals. Following these action steps should help you to find the right volunteer opportunities in the right not-for-profit organization. These steps constitute a planning process that should result in experiences that will make you a truly "Happy Volunteer."

Action Steps to Finding the Right Volunteer Opportunities in the Right Organizations

✔ Decide what are the most important goals that you want to achieve at the present time through the process of volunteering.

✔ Develop a list of specific not-for-profit organizations that can provide you, as a volunteer, with the best environment to reach your goals. Use the "Personal Values and Preferences Work Environment Inventory" and the "Initial Organization Identification Guide," which follow, to help you in this process.

✔ From this list, identify the two or three organizations that you believe will best enable you to reach your goals for the volunteer experience.

✔ Next evaluate each of these organizations using the factors identified in the "Organizational Analysis Guide Concerning Volunteer Involvement," which appears below.

✔ Visit and have a personal interview with each of the organizations that remain on your list.

✔ Decide in which of these organizations you would like to volunteer or decide to move on and consider other not-for-profit organizations.

When deciding what are the most important goals that you want to achieve at the present time through the process of volunteering:

• Be certain that the goals are of the first importance to you. The more important, the more motivating they will be.

- Make your goals as concrete as possible.

- Picture the personal enrichment benefits that will occur upon the realization of your goals.

- Identify the resources you will require to help yourself achieve your goals.

- Don't get side-tracked. Keep your goals continuously in mind.

- Talk about your goals and their importance to you with other people. This will help solidify and clarify them and keep you excited and interested.

When developing a list of specific not-for-profit organizations that can provide you, as a volunteer, with the best environment to reach your goals, use the "Personal Values and Preferences Work Environment Inventory" and the "Initial Organization Identification Guide," both of which appear below, to help you in this process.

Each of us has different values and preferences concerning the kind of environment in which we like to work. Prior to developing a list of specific not-for-profit organizations that you believe can provide you, as a volunteer, with the best environment to reach your goals, it is important that you carefully consider your values and preferences concerning the work environment.

The following inventory should prove helpful in this process. Place a checkmark in the appropriate column after each statement which best describes the importance that you attach to that particular aspect of the work environment. A clear understanding of your values and preferences concerning a supportive work environment will help you to locate the kinds of organizations that will be most productive for you in maximizing the benefits of the volunteer experience and making you a truly "Happy Volunteer."

Personal Values and Preferences Work Environment Inventory			
How Important Are the Following Aspects of the Work Environment to Me?	Important	Somewhat Important	Not Important
Size of the Organization			
Degree of Formality / Informality			
Opportunity to Work Alone			
Opportunity to Work in Groups			
Scope of Responsibility			
Scope of Authority			
Opportunity to be Creative and Innovative			
Opportunity to Contribute Your Ideas			
Opportunity to Make Decisions			
Opportunity to Receive Feedback Concerning Your Performance			
Opportunity to Receive Recognition for the Work You Do			
Opportunity to Be Part of a Supportive Work Group			
Opportunity to Do Work that Makes a Difference			
Having a Supportive Boss			
The Personal Characteristics of Your Boss			
Having Direct Involvement with Clients			
Having Direct Involvement with the Community			
Having Access to Experts in the Field			
Being Able to Participate in a Range of Projects			

After you have thought about and completed the "Personal Values and Preferences Work Environment Inventory," you are ready to proceed to develop your list of specific not-for-profit organizations that you believe can provide you with the best environment to reach your goals as a volunteer. The "Initial Organization Identification Guide" which follows should help you to create this list.

Initial Organization Identification Guide

Are you excited about the mission of the organization? Do you find the mission compelling and of special interest to you?

What is the field of activity in which this not-for-profit organization is primarily involved:

❏ The Arts   ❏ Health Related

❏ Athletics/Recreation   ❏ Political

❏ Business   ❏ Religious/Spiritual

❏ Education   ❏ Social Service

❏ The Environment

Is this field of activity important and of special interest to you at this time?

What are the areas of special emphasis of this organization within the broad fields of activity identified above? Are these areas of special emphasis of compelling interest and importance to you?

What is the track record of this organization with regard to the participation of volunteers? Is this organization supportive of volunteer involvement?

continues next page

Initial Organization Identification Guide

continued

How accessible is this organization and its opportunities to you as a volunteer?

Do the size and organizational structure of this organization enhance the volunteer experiences which are available to you?

What is the reputation of this organization as an employer? Is the personal growth and development of employees a central concern? Is this a learning organization?

What is the professional reputation of this organization?

What is the reputation of this organization in the community?

After you have identified the two or three organizations from your initial list of not-for-profit organizations that you believe will best enable you to reach your goals as a volunteer, evaluate each of these organizations using the factors identified in the "Organizational Analysis Guide Concerning Volunteer Involvement," which appears below.

Organizational Analysis Guide Concerning Volunteer Involvement

An organization's attitude concerning the importance of volunteers in helping to achieve its mission should be of central importance in your decision concerning the place where you want to volunteer. Asking and answering the questions contained in the "Organizational Analysis Guide Concerning Volunteer Involvement" which appears below should prove useful in assessing this attitude.

Organizational Analysis Guide Concerning Volunteer Involvement		
	Yes	No
Are volunteers mentioned in the mission statement?		
Is there a published statement about the role of volunteers in the organization?		
Are the contributions of volunteers mentioned in the annual report?		
Are volunteers perceived as full-fledged members of the staff?		
Is there a strong track record of volunteer contribution in the organization?		
Is there a significant number of volunteers currently involved in the organization?		
Is there a coordinator of volunteers position?		
Are the members of the board of directors respected contributors to the community?		
Do the members of the volunteer board of directors demonstrate the importance of the contributions of volunteers?		
Are there training and other educational programs available for volunteers?		

Following your evaluation using the "Organizational Analysis Guide Concerning Volunteer Involvement," schedule a visit and personal interview with each of the organizations that remain on your list of places in which you may be interested in volunteering. Suggestions concerning the kinds of questions and issues you might want to ask and discuss are described below. These questions and issues all relate to the status of volunteers in the organization.

Possible Questions to Ask in Your Personal Visit and Interview

Status of Volunteers

- How are the efforts of volunteers coordinated in the organization?
- Do volunteers have employment contracts? If so what is included in these contracts?
- How is the performance of volunteers evaluated?
- How are volunteers and volunteer performance recognized?
- Can volunteers be promoted?
- Is there a suggestion system for volunteers?

Nature of Work

- How much flexibility is there in working hours?
- How much flexibility is there in working locations?
- What is the extent of the participation of volunteers in decision-making?
- What opportunity is there to experience different jobs?

- How does a volunteer move from one assignment to another assignment?
- Does a volunteer have the opportunity to work on assignments from beginning to end?
- Are volunteers encouraged to be innovative?

Relationships with Others

- Do volunteers have the opportunity to work directly with clients?
- Do volunteers have any direct involvement with the community?
- Do volunteers have the opportunity to work directly with other volunteers?
- Do volunteers have the opportunity to work directly with paid employees?
- What is the nature of the volunteer staff – paid staff relationship in the organization?
- Does a volunteer have the opportunity to choose and work with different mentors?

Learning organizations are organizations that value the personal growth and development of their employees. You may want to discuss some of the organizational character- istics which are most important to you, that are identified in the following diagram of a learning organization, in your personal visit and interview with the organizations in which you are considering volunteering.

Characteristics of a Learning Organization

There is an air of exploration and discovery.

People are encouraged, not penalized, for trying new things.

Innovation is rewarded.

Creativity is encouraged.

The external environment is continuously being screened.

Continuing education is part of the culture.

Ideas are highly valued.

Continuous improvement is embedded in the culture.

Change is perceived as continuing and desirable.

The development of human potential is a central concern.

Service and product excellence are demanded.

There is an air of excitement.

Individual expression is encouraged.

The environment is participative in nature.

Useful Resources for Finding the Right Volunteer Opportunities in the Right Organizations

It is possible for you to find valuable, personally rewarding volunteer opportunities which involve the internet and other communication technologies. In some cases the volunteer experience may take place in its entirety over the internet and through other telecommunication devices.

The focus in this book however, is on volunteer participation in which a volunteer is physically present in the environment in which the volunteering takes place during at least part of the volunteer experience. With this fact in mind, it is likely that most volunteer activities will take place within commuting distance of the residence of the volunteer. This distance may vary to some degree, but here the focus is on a 25 to 30 mile radius of the volunteer's home. This is important to keep in mind as the potential volunteer identifies and uses resources to locate the opportunities in the right organization in which to volunteer. The following listing identifies possible resources that may prove useful in this process.

Useful Resources

Resource People

- Current employees
- Clients of the organization
- Members of boards of directors
- Current and past volunteers
- Business associates
- Family, friends, and connecting networks
- Community members
- Suppliers

Communication Sources

- Internet
- Annual reports
- Not-for-profit directories
- Business directories
- Newspapers
- Economic development publications
- Business journals
- Census data
- Not-for-profit organization publications and journals
- Magazines
- Not-for-profit research reports

Organizational Resources

- Libraries
- Chambers of Commerce
- United Ways
- Foundations
- Trade associations
- Councils of churches
- Service clubs
- Elder services
- U.S. Census Bureau
- American Association of Retired Persons
- Not-for-profit organization associations
- Governmental research agencies
- Individual professional not-for-profit membership organizations
- College and university placement offices
- College and university research centers
- Community economic development offices
- Professional volunteer associations

In order for these resources to be really useful they have to identify enriching volunteer opportunities in organizations which match the kind of commitment which you bring to the volunteer experience. For example, if you are able to commit two hours a week to the volunteer experience, this experience must fit that degree of commitment with regard to commuting time, extent of work that can be done at home, on the internet, etc. As a volunteer, you need to be as clear as possible about how much time, energy, and effort you can give to the volunteer experience. The extent of this commitment could, of course, change over a period of time.

A major resource in locating the right volunteer opportunities for you in the right organization can be your family, friends, and their connecting networks with other people. We will call this the "Circle of Exploration and Discovery of Volunteer Opportunities." These networks of interconnecting contacts are often overlooked. They can be an important source for identifying enriching opportunities for you as a volunteer.

To illustrate the power of the "Circle of Exploration and Discovery of Volunteer Opportunities," take a few minutes to think about your own family, friends, and associates and the contacts and potential resource people with whom they interact. It is amazing how this interacting network can fan out to identify the opportunities you are looking for as a volunteer.

Throughout the process of finding the right volunteer opportunities in the right organizations, it is important for you to remember the significance of this process. Finding opportunities in not-for-profit organizations that support and appreciate the contributions of volunteers will go a long way in making your experiences as a volunteer as personally

Wisdom from the
HAPPY VOLUNTEER

"Learning organizations are
organizations that value the
personal growth and development
of their employees."

"It is important that the process of
moving on to new experiences be done
in a responsible manner with
consideration for both the well-being
of you, as a volunteer, and the
organization in which you are
contributing your services."

fulfilling and rewarding as possible. Make the extra effort to find organizations in which you have an excellent opportunity to achieve your goals for the volunteer experience.

Moving On to Enriching, Fulfilling, and Growth-Producing Experiences in a New Not-for-Profit Organization

This book is about moving on to become a volunteer and experiencing the many wonderful, fulfilling, and enriching benefits of the volunteer experience. It is also about moving from one volunteer experience to another as your learning and personal enrichment needs change with different stages of your development as a person.

Moving on as a volunteer involves knowing how to get started and knowing when and how to move to new situations both within the same organization and in new organizational settings.

It is important that the process of moving on to new experiences be done in a responsible manner with consideration for both the well-being of you, as a volunteer, and the organization in which you are contributing your services. Some indicators that it may be time for you to move on to a new set of volunteer experiences are included as part of our discussion of this issue. You may be able to change some of the negative indicators which are mentioned, but if several of them continue to be present it will probably be desirable for you to make a change. If this is the case, suggestions for moving to new volunteer opportunities in different organizations are also included.

Remember that you, as a volunteer, have choices as to where you will be a volunteer and that volunteers are always in demand. If you are to be the "Happy Volunteer," it is essential that you find your volunteer experiences fulfilling, rewarding, and enriching. Knowing when and how to move on to new experiences is a critical part of the process of being a "Happy Volunteer" who, in turn, contributes to the happiness of the clients of the organization in which he or she is volunteering.

How do you know when to move on to new volunteer experiences?

- You have lost your sense of excitement.
- You no longer look forward to going to work at your volunteer assignments.
- You are unable to meet learning goals that are important to you.
- You are not encouraged to learn new things.
- Your input and ideas are not solicited.
- You are no longer encouraged to experiment with new ways of doing things.
- You are not receiving useful feedback concerning your performance.
- The mission of the organization no longer resonates with you.
- You are bored with the work you are doing.
- The work you are doing is not important.
- The work you are doing is not challenging and stimulating.

Suggestions concerning moving on to new volunteer opportunities in a new organization

- See if you can negotiate new opportunities in your present organization.

- If you have made the decision to move to another organization as a volunteer, give adequate notice of these plans to the organization in which you are presently volunteering.

- Thank your present organization for providing you with personal growth opportunities in meeting your goals.

- Indicate that you would like to stay in touch with the organization in which you are presently volunteering.

- Indicate that you would greatly appreciate a letter of reference and recommendation from this organization since you value the work it is doing.

- Provide input to the organization that you feel would be helpful and to which the organization would be receptive.

- Leave your current organization in as positive a manner as possible. Make every effort to leave with a good mutual feeling.

- After you have left, refrain from making negative comments about the organization that has provided you with volunteer opportunities.

Being a Happy Volunteer

Questions to ask yourself after reading this chapter:

- What are the action steps for finding the right volunteer opportunities in the right organizations?

- What can you do to make your goals for the volunteer experience as personally motivating as possible?

- What are your values and preferences concerning the work environment in which you volunteer?

- What are some important questions to ask in order to identify an initial list of not-for-profit organizations in which you might want to volunteer?

- What are the specific questions that you would ask about the involvement and participation of volunteers that are important to you?

- What are the characteristics of a learning organization?

- What resources do you plan to use in order to find the right volunteer opportunities in the right organization for you?

- What are your thoughts about how you will move on to new volunteer experiences in a manner that is mutually beneficial to you, as a volunteer, and to the organization in which you are volunteering?

Conclusion

The Happy Volunteer Challenge

It is the hope of the author that you will make the decision to become the Happy Volunteer as a result of reading this book.

This book has focused on the many personal benefits that you will receive as a volunteer in a not-for-profit organization. Volunteering in public and private sector organizations can also be highly worthwhile. Volunteering is a wonderful way to realize your personal enrichment goals, career goals, and life goals.

The volunteer experience can be of great benefit to you at different stages of your life. These experiences can provide you with the joy, happiness, and sense of personal worth and meaning that are essential to living a productive and rewarding life. Through the volunteer experience you have the opportunity to build on your personal strengths and use them to achieve greater happiness and personal fulfillment while helping others.

The author urges you to live a more fulfilling and rewarding life by becoming part of the great American tradition of volunteering. He urges you to become the Happy Volunteer!